Sam Gary,

Son of a SEACOOK!

By: Sam Gary

Copyright © 2021 by Sam Hofer Sr.

All rights reserved, including the right to reproduce this book or portions thereof in any form whatsoever or by any means. No part of this book may be reproduced, stored in a retrieval system, or transmitted by any means without the written permission of the Author, except as provided by United States of America copyright law.

First Paperback Edition May 2021

Scriptures referred to in this book are taken from the most up to date translations of the Holy Bible published by Zondervan Publishing House and provided online by Biblegateway.com. Some names have been changed to protect individuals and their rights.

Cover Picture Credits belong to Sam's seven-year-old granddaughters, Brookie and Rihanna.

Drawing credits of The Black Stallion & Eeyore belong to Becca Ramer.

Manufactured in the United States of America

Published by Victory Vision Publishing
& Consulting, LLC

www.victoryvision.org

ISBN: 9798746422682

Bedtime was a favorite growing up. Dad would strum his guitar and sing *"Strawberry Roan," "Bismarck," "Old Log Cabin,"* and many more oldies while we climbed into our PJ's excited for story time. We'd pile on Mom and Dad's bed, suggesting all our favorite tales. Dad had a stuffed fox who was the puppet for so many hair-raising stories of Peter Rabbit and his 101 ways to evade Reddy and Granny Fox. Our eyes as wide as saucers, I can hear to this day Reddy's "voice" through Dad, as he planned Peter's downfall.

As much as we lived for those bedtime tales, our favorite stories of all were those Dad told of his growing up years. Wild and free, all the cousins lived together on a huge farm in the middle of the open prairie. Mischief and adventure were served up daily.

We loved the story of the time when they put an innertube around the pony's neck, attached baler twine to said inner tube, and from there to the little red wagon tongue. Perched inside the wagon was a child ready to have a 'buggy' ride. It didn't end as the imagination had pictured. You could find us targeting Auntie's ducks with slingshots, rafting down the canal like Huck Finn and Tom Sawyer, bucking out wild broncs on a dare, slopping out hundreds of pigs before school, combining thousands of acres each fall and all the adventures that happened each harvest time.

As we grew older, the stories broadened—a motor quitting in the middle of the ocean late at night, swimming at dusk in the everglades to push a boat home, accidentally taking out an entire town's lights with a harvester, locking the preacher in the outhouse, rounding up cattle off the prairie for branding, being chased by a bull, and so much more.

Dad was famous for his stories. Many a Saturday night, our house was full of young people. Mom had food and coffee for everyone, and Dad has his guitar and stories. It was always a hit.

Anywhere we went, people would ask for the stories they loved best. Many nights after supper with friends, the evening would turn into, *"Sam, tell us about the time you…"* and we'd all lean forward with anticipation.

For years we have begged Dad to write his stories. They are treasures of times past. Laugh till you cry. Feel every emotion of an era gone by. Hold your breath, waiting in anticipation for what is next, or wipe a tear wishing you could turn back the hands of time when kids were kids outdoors.

Thousands are waiting for this book, knowing many of the favorite stories they've heard over the years are inside. I look at it as a legacy Dad is writing for us. It started in my heart as a little girl in her PJ's waiting for story time with Daddy!

~Jessica

CONTENTS

	Acknowledgments	i
	Endorsements	iii
1	SON OF A SEACOOK	1
2	THE GREAT CELL PHONE FISHING TRIP	7
3	ALL IT TOOK WAS AN OLD SOW	19
4	THE TEMPTATION TO GET BENT OUT OF SHAPE	25
5	MY GOD, THERE'S A LOT OF BENS	31
6	JOJO'S BLACK STALLIONS	39
7	CON MAN	51
8	THE DANGERS OF LEAVING YOUR HUBBY HOME ALONE	71
9	CHINOOK WIND	81
10	LOS ANGELES – HAROLD & I	91
11	RIGHTEOUS JIM	99
12	THE HOUSE THAT JACK BUILT	107
13	BOTTOMLESS WHISKEY	113
14	STRAINING AT A GNAT	119
15	TALK IS CHEAP	125
16	SUPERNATURAL CONNECTION	135
17	BULLS & HEIFERS	141
18	A HOUSE FULL OF LADIES	147
19	DESPERATE CIRCUMSTANCES	157
20	BRIEFCASE	161
21	24 ¼ BY 17 ½	169
22	SPIRITUAL ILLUSIONS	173
23	TOILET PAPER THIEF	177
24	GETTING RID OF THE GREEN	183
25	A TWENTY-FIVE YEAR OLD GUILTY CONSCIENCE	189
26	NEVER SAY "WHOA" IN A MUDHOLE	193
27	WHEN GIVING DOESN'T MAKE SENSE	205
	About the Author	219
	Bibliography	221

ACKNOWLEDGEMENTS

Son of a Seacook has taken me a considerable amount of time to write, and the task has been personally rewarding and a lot of fun at the same time. I want to thank the following people whose various contributions have made it all possible.

My first and deepest thank you goes to my awesome wife and best friend, Joanie, who has faithfully and unflinchingly supported me during the writing of this book. She listened to the stories and rewarded me with understanding and genuine laughter. It kept me going!

My warmest thank you goes to each of our incredible children—Jessica Marie, Jacquelyn Gail, Jolane Dawn, and Samuel George, for insisting that I write these stories out and compile them in a book. They are my biggest fans!

Thank you to my sister, Ruth Ann Stelfox, and our friends, Katrina Yoder and Kim Mast, for their extraordinary work of editing the rough copies and making the sentences flow. I know it was hard work, and I am grateful.

Thank you to my publisher and friend, Julie Ballard (Victory Vision), for your invaluable feedback and your professional touches on the finished copy. Your outstanding contributions are much appreciated.

I am truly thankful for the many others who have encouraged me, supported me, and made this an experience of a lifetime!

Sincerely, Sam Gary

ENDORSEMENTS

In the decades I have known Sam, I can honestly say he never ceases to amaze me—a great and loyal friend and an extremely intelligent and talented man. Sam has tirelessly moved from one career to another. A man after God's own heart, Sam has been living out the dreams of not only myself, but many others with no signs of slowing down. He has gone from farming to building pontoon boats, singer/songwriter/recording artist, pilot (just to name a few), and now to his new endeavor of publishing this wonderful book. I'm not sure how he does it, but I get tired just thinking about all he has accomplished. Sam has an uncanny way of drawing his readers into his world. His positive, infectious sense of humor lends nicely to his retelling of these wonderful personal stories, which will certainly entertain and amuse all readers.

My best wishes and God's blessings go out to Sam, his beautiful wife, and his amazing family.

Brent D. Austin
Warrant Officer (Ret'd.)
Canadian Armed Forces, Military Police

It reminds you of all the forgotten yesteryears that were so full of compelling lessons, all told with a surprising twist of humor! My brother cannot refrain from telling others about Jesus, so He is found in most of these true stories! You will be charmed and amused by this delightful collection of real, down-to-earth tales from Sam's incredible wealth of memories!

Ruth Ann Stelfox
Author of "Tears Of the Rain" and "Joey's Story"

I first met Sam when I was 17. His stories, experiences, and insights both transfixed and inspired me at a critical time in my life. Time has proven that his passion for Jesus and radical commitment to the Kingdom of God is not just a passing whim; his flame continues to burn white-hot, piercing the darkness of this world. Completely transformed by Jesus, Sam has been used by God to touch thousands of lives through song and sermon, whether from the stage or over the CB radio. To date, Sam has been one of my greatest mentors and friends. May his tribe increase to the glory of God as these stories get retold over and over again!

Luke Kuepfer
Speaker | Author | Life Coach

I first met Sam Gary when I was 17 years old. The stories in this book will give you a glimpse at how genuine and authentic he is as a man, husband, father, grandpa, and Christian! This book is written in a way that anyone can relate to, no matter what your background is!

Al Bontrager
Owner of Silver Ridge Construction, LLC

I have known Sam for over 20 years. He has blessed my life in many ways. I have vacationed with, worked with, played with, and partied with Sam. His family is like family to me. He is a phenomenal storyteller. I have heard a lot of these stories over the years, and I can't wait for you to read this book—one minute, you will be laughing until your sides hurt, and the next, crying from the tremendous emotion of the story. I know you will feel like you're living in the moment and wonder how one person has lived through so many fascinating events. Sam lives life to the fullest, and his heart is as big as Texas. I'm sure you will see that played out through the following chapters.

Treva Ann
Accountant and Business Owner

I have known Sam for the better part of 20 years. Sam is a man of character and integrity. I learned many things from him; one of the greatest is that he "be real."

Sam is one of the most honorable men I have ever met. I have worked alongside him. I played in a band and traveled with him. I laughed with and cried with him. I have seen him down and seen him up.

The stories he shares here are funny, sobering, and emotional—many times within a few lines. There are many life lessons in these stories that are easy to identify with. These stories have shown me that life is a series of stepping stones that, if we don't stumble on them, will take us to greater heights in life. We choose to be the victim or the Victor!

Dr. Leland Hershey

SON OF A SEACOOK

Back when I still lived on the family farm, there was a neighbor of ours, a Mr. Bert, who I would sometimes go work for when his workload got too heavy; usually around springtime, calving season, or fall harvest. He was one of the most decent, respectful gentlemen I've ever run across. To this day, forty years later, I still think the world of Mr. Bert. He was a real community changer who did a lot of good for our county as an active member on many local boards.

This fine gentleman's father, Alex, was a giant of a man with massive, hairy arms and a chest that made other men look like little immature schoolboys. He also had an explosive temper, much larger than his stature, and seemingly uncontrollable. Once or twice a month, when he would blow a fuse and curse his one-and-only son, the neighbors on both sides of his farm could hear his booming voice, even though they lived a half a mile away. Whenever that violent storm would strike, the poor soul he was standing next to would feel the pain of his explosions verbally, physically, and emotionally.

One fine summer day, I happened to be standing next to Alex as we were both leaning over the hood of his pickup. Bert was sitting nearby on a tractor and had been conversing with his father in as friendly and respectful a manner as anyone ever could have. Minutes later, Bert happened to disagree with his father on some point they were discussing, and the explosion occurred. Alex's boiler suddenly overheated, and his safety valve blew. I'm telling you, if a 9.0 magnitude earthquake had taken place, I couldn't have been more shocked than I was watching that scene unfold in front of me on that sizzling hot summer day. I dare say that old '79 single cab pickup truck was built Ford-tough, probably twice as tough as today's new trucks, but it was no match for the blows of this man's clenched fists. They rained down mercilessly for two or three minutes on its unsuspecting surface and permanently caved in the hood, the sub stiffeners, and the top ridge of that poor old F-150.

He cursed his offspring so hard and twisted Christ Jesus' name into his sentences so savagely and profanely, that my body involuntarily started moving away from him. I shuffled backward in a Michael-Jackson-style moonwalk, almost sure the ground would open at any moment and swallow him alive. I've seen people lose it before, and I've seen people lose it since, but never in all my days have I seen such a violent reaction. I imagine his adrenaline levels made him feel invincible, like the soldiers who used to fight in hand-to-hand combat and were able to ignore the worst kind of pain. Come to think of it, I am sure his wrists were sore for a week after the adrenaline wore off.

Anyway, after this horrible, blasphemous outburst, Alex climbed into his freshly-branded, severely-dented Ford and left the scene. I looked at his son, Bert, and asked, "How on earth can you handle that coming from your very own father and not say a single word? Is this the first time it's happened?" Apparently, it had been this way for as long as Bert could remember, and he learned just to let it blow over like a passing thunderstorm and not take it to heart. That was a mighty strange concept to me, but you learn something new every day.

I guess this is why I have the utmost respect for this gentleman. Through his example, I've learned how to properly respond to some bad situations I've found myself in over the years, without saying a word in retaliation. Proverbs says that even a fool is thought to be wise when he keeps his mouth shut. One of the greatest, most effective weapons of life is to just walk away and be quiet when someone does you wrong. Speak neither good nor bad. Folks can't stand it when they don't know what you're thinking, and when their malicious actions can't get a rise out of you.

People may advise you to stay away from a man who has such a temperamental father; after all, like father, like son. But in this case, that saying doesn't hold true. I've seen quite a few sons whose fathers were total jerks...alcoholics, cheats, and the whole gamut of terrible things, but these sons have entirely broken the vicious cycle of failure to become the most honorable of men.

At any rate, I was shocked at hearing the name of Jesus Christ desecrated in such a horrible, twisted fashion. My own father never said anything above the level of "damn," "what the hell," or "bastard," and it was probably warranted at the time. So, this type of railing, cursing, and blaspheming, with its many descriptive four-letter words gushing forth from Mr. Alex, actually scared me something powerful. I said to my poor neighbor, whom I now truly pitied, "I'm not going to work here anymore if your dad comes around here and curses like he just did, using the name of Jesus Christ in his sordid mixture of blasphemy!"

Well, Bert must've gone right home and told his father what I had said. The very next morning, bright and early, there came that old, green, 1979 Ford F-150, sporting its newly acquired style of concaved hood. Out stepped Mr. Alex, looking bigger and burlier than he had the day before. I could hear my heart pounding in my ears as he walked towards me. He put that massive, hairy arm around my shoulder and pulled me tightly to himself. He put his face about four inches from mine, so close that I could see his eyes brimming with tears, as he told me he was S-O-O-O sorry for losing his temper, and for using God's name in such a violent, wicked manner, and that he knew it was all wrong to do so. Then, as he awkwardly continued to hold me close to himself, he asked in the sincerest voice, "Would it be all right if I would just say '*son of a seacook*' from now on, instead of 'Jesus Christ'?"

I stood there dumbfounded in this tight embrace, with my mouth hanging open, but no words came. I mean, *hokey-doodle*, here was this giant of a man, now cool as a cucumber, seemingly harmless as a big teddy bear, holding me in a vice-like grip and asking me if he could change his cursing vocabulary to '*son of a seacook*'! We stood that way, locked together, one willing, the other with no other choice, for what seemed like a small eternity. All the while, I just nodded my head up and down like it was on a mechanical spring. Finally, he let me go. He told me to jump into his truck, and at a blistering speed of forty miles an hour, in what seemed to be a state of sober contemplation, he drove me five miles to the local dairy bar and bought us both giant vanilla milkshakes.

As we were driving back to the farm, he said, "I have one more confession I'd like to make, if you don't mind listening."

"Go ahead," I said, now starting to feel somewhat like a priest must feel at confession. Looking back now, my friend was Roman Catholic, so everything was almost in order, except that it was now an unordained, Gentile priest doing the listening. Ha-ha! I didn't know what was coming down the tube, so I just let him talk!

"Well," he began, "a while back, I was diagnosed with terminal cancer, and because I've done nothing more than work all my life, I had a considerable amount of money saved up. Know what I did?"

"Tell me," I said.

"I figured if I'm dying anyway, then what the hell? I might as well try gambling, and if I win, my family will love me. If I lose, they'll hate me, but I'll be dead, so what does it matter? Dammit anyhow, know what ended up happening? I lost all the money, and son of a b------, I ended up not dying, and now my family won't even speak to me!"

I just stared at him for a long time and finally said, "Son of a seacook, you've got yourself in a horrible fix." He just kept looking straight ahead and sipped his vanilla milkshake 'til we got back to the farm.

A little something I've learned over the years is when you don't stay in your own little bubble and you reach into other people's lives, at least there's no such thing as a dull day or a boring life! The thought just hit me right now that maybe this is what Jesus meant when He told us to follow Him and we'd get to experience the abundant life! I was always hoping it meant that we'd get lots of money! Ha-ha!

If we are the light of the world, then it doesn't matter how dark the darkness is; the light will shine all the brighter. But I'll let you guys all draw your own conclusions, or parallels, or life's lessons.

From that day on, Mr. Alex and I were excellent friends. He would frequently phone me and tell me about the good sermons he had listened to and ask what I thought about them. He would drive into my yard on hot summer days, come inside my shop, sit down on a chair, and fall asleep. He said it was the coolest building in the county, and he hoped I didn't mind. I expect to see my dear friend someday, over yonder, in a new Heaven and a new Earth, where God will wipe away all tears from our eyes, and we will experience nothing but love.

After telling my cousins and my local friends my *"Son of a Seacook"* story, the phrase swept through the local gang like wildfire. It never failed to bring the user a big smile. I should have put a trademark on it because *"Son of a Seacook"* became the favorite, most chosen, and most preferred cuss word of the day. Some 45 years later, it is still used on the windswept prairies of southern Alberta, Canada.

THE GREAT CELL PHONE FISHING TRIP

Before I begin this tale, I must tell thee it is not fiction. Nor is it, as one of my cousins from yesteryear would have put it, *"another western."* No! It is the truth, the whole truth, and nothing but the truth, so help me, dear old Aunt Sara. There's an old saying that's been floating around for as long as I can remember: *"Truth is stranger than fiction."* I've found this to be true on several occasions. Some of the things I've experienced have been rather far out, like the time God helped me find my cell phone.

This story takes place in northern Michigan in 2001, shortly after the twin towers fell in New York City. With my oldest daughter recently married and moved away, I had three half-grown kids (ages 19, 16, and 12) still at home. I asked my young son if he'd like to help me do some weed-eating around the large, 300-acre grass pasture we had rented for our horses. Once we finished weed-eating, I promised we'd do some fishing at the bass pond situated at the far end of the field. This suited him just fine, and he was raring to go. About three hours later, with all our weed work done, we immediately headed to our favorite fishing hole at the far end of the 300-acre, knee-high, mosquito-infested, green, waving, ready-to-be-mowed field.

As we started our trek to the far end of the field, I asked my son, "Sammy, can you please tend to the cell phone?" It was an old, prepaid, flip-lid, walkie-talkie-looking thing. I reminded him several times not to lose it, for it was the Cadillac of its time.

"You don't have to worry about me losing this old cell phone," he said with a big grin on his face. "It's in my deepest pocket." With that, he patted his pant leg just above his knee cap, assuring me he had shoved it into his pocket as deep as it could go.

Now, fishing in this spot was truly amazing. Every time you threw in a line, you'd catch a fish! We spent a couple of hours in this little paradise, then started our long walk home through clouds of hungry mosquitoes, hurrying as fast as our feet could carry us. "Hey son, could you please give me the cell phone? I need to call Mom," I said.

I watched what would soon become a familiar scene, which I call the "Attempt of Desperation." In an act of insanity, he did this patting motion right above his kneecap, trying to locate what he already knew was lost, he just couldn't admit it. He continued the fruitless motions, trying to alleviate some unmet need in his soul, which was probably there because his mom didn't change his diapers quick enough, and he still hadn't gotten over it.

Sam says, "The difference between a father-in-law and a son-in-law!"

Finally, my son reached his hand deep into his empty pocket (almost up to his elbow), and sure enough, there was no phone down there. He frantically resumed the fruitless patting motion, this time well below his kneecap, desperate to find the missing cell phone that was lying somewhere in a 300-acre field of knee-high grass. "I'm so sorry, Dad," he said, "I just don't know how that's possible. Maybe if we pray, God will help us find the phone!"

"Yeah, right," I said. "We'll never find it in a million years! And the mosquitoes are driving me mad!"

But, since I had just preached on how big God is and how nothing is too hard for Him, I couldn't very well do anything but pray. It's so easy to talk about faith when you have it for someone else or on a Sunday morning. But, when things get down and dirty, and we're personally at risk, we tend to think a little differently. It's like this one joke I read called *Have Faith My Child.* It goes something like this...

> **For the umpteenth time, Mrs. Faust came to her pastor to tell him, "I'm so scared! My husband, Dan, says he's going to kill me if I continue to come to your church."**
>
> **"Yes, yes, my child," replied the pastor, more than a little tired of hearing this over and over. "I will continue to pray for you, Mrs. Faust. Have faith - the Lord will watch over you."**
>
> **"Oh yes, he has kept me safe thus far, only..."**
>
> **"Only what, my child?"**
>
> **"Well, now he says if I keep coming to your church, he's going to kill YOU!"**
>
> **"Well, now," said the pastor, "Perhaps it's time for you to check out that little church on the other side of town."**

So, now that our faith was put to the test, we bowed our heads, and asked God to help us. Believe it or not, after walking about a quarter-mile, trying to imagine where we had walked before, we spotted the cell phone lying in the tall grass. What's the probability of that happening? I want to tell you, we were ecstatic! Our faith was on a roll, and we were a-rockin'. We were telling everyone about our lost and found! Our faith went from the valley to the mountain top like an F-16 fighter jet, with the afterburners on full throttle.

The next evening, my beautiful and talented middle daughter Jackie came up to me and said, "Dad, if you and I go up to check the horses, maybe we could go spend some time fishing. It's been so long since we've done that, and I think it would be a perfect night. Remember how we used to always go fishing back when we lived in Alberta?" Then she gave me a big smile. Well, what's a man to do? It had just rained a bushel, and in order to get to the fishing hole, we needed to walk the longest length of the field. Thinking it would be some excellent time with my now-eldest daughter still living at home, and thinking I'd have some time to do a little burrowing into her mind, I decided a long walk would be right in order.

After soaking in insect repellent, Jackie and I headed off for an evening adventure. "Now, you listen carefully to me, Jackie," I said, "I'm going to let you take care of the old cell phone, and I'll carry the fishing tackle. But remember, Sammy lost it last night, and I don't want to lose it again. The Lord doesn't help people who aren't careful," I muttered.

"Look here, Dad, I'm going to put this in my front pocket where I can always feel it." And with that, she patted a bulge just above her knee cap.

"That's just what Sammy did last night," I said, "and he lost it."

"Come on, Dad, you just worry too much. You're acting like I'm a two-year-old. It can't fall out of here," and she smiled again.

A smile will disarm me, melt my heart, and get to me faster than most anything. I don't want to go on some long rabbit trail, but do you remember the old ad they used to run for the *Camel* cigarette company? *"I'd walk a mile for a Camel,"* it said, and showed a box of cigarettes that had a picture of a real camel. Well, I've changed that saying to, *"I'd walk a mile for a smile,"* and I really would. It seems our society is so uptight and stressed out these days, that most of us emanate negativity which creates a very toxic environment. It appears that the law of attraction has been all but lost, and we are so stressed out that we've lost our smile.

But, back to my story. Jackie and I had the most incredible fishing night, and I'm sure we both will remember it for many moons to come. To say she was excited is putting it mildly. The expressions on her face told the story of her feelings as she pulled in the biggest largemouth bass I'd ever seen. We were so excited about this record catch that we didn't even complain about the millions of mosquitoes who were now plunging through the defenses of our insect repellent trying to get more of the sweetest blood they'd ever tasted. Then, as the sun was beginning to set, we both raced as fast as we could to get to the safety of the truck and rid ourselves of the horrible man-eating plague of mosquitoes.

"Wow!" Jackie said, "Thanks a lot, Dad! This sure was one of our better fishing trips. What an awesome night!"

"It sure was," I agreed. "It's an awesome memory we just built tonight, and I can't wait to tell the rest of the family about that big bass you landed. Let me see the cell phone so that I can do a little fish-bragging."

My mouth hung open in unbelief as Jackie began to do the leg-patting thing, which I instantly dreaded. She also patted just below the kneecap just to make sure it was really lost!!!

"Dad!" she said, with the most sheepish, greenish, longish expression that she could muster. "Dad! It's gone; it's not here!" That dang-blasted, blankety-blank of an old, prepaid, flip-lid, walkie-talkie-looking cell phone was lying somewhere between the 300-acre, knee-high, mosquito-infested, green, waving, ready-to-be-mowed, field and our truck.

"What should we do, Dad? It's much too dark to see anything if we try to backtrack, and I'm sure we'd never find it if we did." To say the least, I was ticked. I was upset. And, I was in no mood to walk two more miles without a chance of ever finding my now jinxed cell phone. All my excitement from the night before and the desire to tell the miracle of the lost-and-found cell phone was gone. It was so ridiculous that I didn't want anyone to even hear about it.

The Great Cell Phone Fishing Trip

Then, I heard this soft voice speaking behind me, "Dad, if you will just pray, I will walk back down to the pond and see if I can find it." And as my daughter walked the long way back, I sat and prayed. Finally, after about three-quarters of an hour, I could make out her silhouette walking towards me. Jackie got in the truck, and with a sheepish smirk, held up my cell phone.

"Wow," I said, "how did you ever find that thing?"

"I prayed all the way back to the fishing hole, and I looked down at the ground and caught a glimpse of something in the grass. I reached down, and there it was."

"Praise ye the Lord," I said.

This was so humbling that it just completely sobered me. It was very, very quiet as we drove the fifteen miles home. I felt like a total unbeliever, or perhaps like one of the unbelieving Israelites that God had to destroy in the wilderness because of their wretchedness.

After some reflection, I did my best to promise God I'd never doubt Him again. It was a shake-yourself-off, try-again, recommit moment, if I'd ever had one. I was *so* committed to trying harder, I hoped I wouldn't blow it again.

When Jackie and I got back to the house, my youngest daughter, Jolane, walked in. Spotting the huge largemouth bass and smiling at me, she said, "Dad, when are you going to take me fishing? You take everybody else." Well, this being my youngest daughter at the time, I figured, "Here's another perfect opportunity to speak into her life." So, I told her all about how big my God was and the marvelous answers to prayer. She said, "Man, God sure is wonderful. He has worlds and universes to take care of, but still messes around with insignificant things like cell phones." I slept well that night, just meditating on the goodness of my Lord.

The next evening, Jolane and I were on the way to the 300-acre, knee-high, mosquito-infested, green, waving, ready-to-be-mowed field to catch the fish I had missed the night before, which I knew was bigger than Jackie's.

We got to the big field, and I looked with a lingering stare at my third and youngest daughter and said, "Jolane, there is no way on God's good green Earth that I'm letting you carry the old, prepaid, flip-lid, walkie-talkie-looking cell phone. So tonight, you'll help carry the fishing box and fishing tackle, which gets mighty heavy after a mile of pushing through the tall grass."

She just cheerfully picked up the tackle box and said, "Let's go, Dad." With that, she skipped off through the tall grass like a little child, and I found myself running hard just to keep up.

I didn't want to lose the cell phone again, so I'd check to make sure it was in my coat pocket every now and then. We did the long walk and very soon started to pull in fishy after fishy. What an absolute blast; what a perfect time spent with each member of my family. When I finished taking each of our children out fishing, I would take my beautiful wife out to the Red Lobster, so all the needs of fellowship and the circle of love could make another completed round. "Yes, this is truly living," I thought.

There was a little paddle boat by the pond at this time, so I got in and rowed out to the middle of the lake. There was also a compartment located in the center of the boat to place one's belongings so they didn't get lost. I carefully put the old cell phone in the compartment so I wouldn't lose it and enjoyed myself for a while, paddling around the pond. Becoming tired of sitting, I went back to the shore and did some more fishing.

Jolane, seeing the empty boat, climbed in and headed out for the middle. As I looked up and saw her taking the boat, I frantically felt my pockets for the cell phone. With dismay, I realized I had left it in the center of the paddle boat. I figured, "This can't be," but so as not to show my paranoia, I yelled over to Jolane, "Don't lose the cell phone! It's in the middle of the boat."

"I won't lose it, Daddy. I'll just leave it in the boat!" she hollered back.

After fishing off the boat for about an hour, Jolane docked it on the opposite shore of the lake and started to fish her way back towards me. "Don't forget the phone," I yelled once again, just for safety's sake.

"I won't," Jolane yelled back. "It's here in my front pocket." With that, she patted her leg just above the kneecap.

At this point, I knew we'd passed the danger stage and were relatively safe. I was positive it wouldn't be lost again, but the thought of it happening was absurd. It just couldn't, and we knew in our hearts that even Murphy's Law wouldn't allow such a thing. Jolane walked slowly around the lake, fishing all the while. When she returned, it was getting dark, so we needed to head out.

"Give me the phone, Jolane," I said. "I'm not taking any chances having you carry it through the field."

Do you have any idea what I felt like when she started patting her leg and checking below her knee caps? "I just had it, Daddy!!"

At this point, I lost it. I sinned. I said things that would make a saint blush. It was just too much! It just couldn't be, but it was true. I was sure it was even too much for God. I knew He knew where it was, but I was not going to ask Him. I was far too upset to pray. The chance of finding this crazy phone again was slimmer than the nostril hairs of a gnat, living inside a log on the backside of a lousy, Louisiana swamp. It was just too much, even for a righteous man to take.

That little voice in my head kept saying, "All you really need to do is apologize to your daughter and pray again, and I'll show you where it is." But oh, how terrible pride is. I blew it again. I failed again. I broke my promise to God again. "Dear Lord," I prayed as my head fell on my chest, "be merciful to me, a sinner. Forgive me the words and the anger I just unleashed on my wonderful daughter. Please, God, for Jesus' sake, forgive me again?"

It all looked so hopeless this time. The grass around the lake was up to three feet tall; it was so much higher. The phone could have fallen into the lake because Jolane was so close to the shore. It probably fell into the water when she got out of the boat. The bottom line was, I just never felt like bringing the same dumb insignificant problem to God for the third night in a row.

The Great Cell Phone Fishing Trip

Does an earthly king help a peasant dig through the mud to find her lost coin?

Does the King of Kings and Lord of Lords who sits in the heavens, Who watches every starving child, Who sees every murder take place, Who feels the pain of all the persecuted Christians suffering in all the countries of the world, really care if I, living here in America, in the land of plenty, lost my stupid cell phone for the third night in a row?

As I walked back and forth dealing with my emotions, I had the feeling that God was laughing at me. Because I was fighting anger again on my inside, I was *so* tempted to lash out again, but instead, I prayed and just hurt over my spiritual immaturity. Then, I walked 100 feet, looked down, and there it lay. Praise ye the Lord!

Often in life, we blame the devil for things, or we wonder if God is just testing us. But we won't get answers to a lot of our questions until we can ask God in eternity. Even then, who knows if we'll even remember them or care about them?

I don't know why I had to lose my cell phone three nights in a row, but I do know that it taught me a valuable lesson: God cares for me and my needs, even the smallest ones. I guess He has a sense of humor since He uses unconventional methods to get us to trust Him sometimes. It reminds me of another story I once heard.

> *An elderly lady was well-known for her faith and for her boldness in talking about it. She would stand on her front porch and shout, "PRAISE THE LORD!"*
>
> *Next door to her lived an atheist who would get so angry at her proclamations he would shout, "There ain't no Lord!!*
>
> *Hard times set in on the elderly lady, and she prayed for God to send her some assistance. She stood on her porch and shouted, "PRAISE THE LORD! GOD, I NEED FOOD!! I AM HAVING A HARD TIME. PLEASE, LORD, SEND ME SOME GROCERIES!!"*
>
> *The next morning the lady went out on her porch, noted a large bag of groceries, and shouted, "PRAISE THE LORD!"*

The neighbor jumped from behind a bush and said, "Aha! I told you there was no God! I bought those groceries; God didn't."

The lady started jumping up and down and clapping her hands and said, "PRAISE THE LORD! He not only sent me groceries, but He made the devil pay for them. Praise the Lord!"

What's the moral of the lost cell phone story?

1. Does God have a sense of humor? Maybe.
2. Does God answer prayer? Ya, this could be it.
3. Never give up repenting? Never.
4. Does a good man fall seven times? The perfect number.
5. Always fight from a place of victory because the battle has been won.
6. Don't take these temporal things too seriously.
7. I know!! Truth is stranger than fiction. Ha! Love ya all.

ALL IT TOOK WAS AN OLD SOW

I remember those hot summer days when my dad and I would work in front of the mechanic shop where he spent a lot of his time. It was usually too hot to work inside the shop, and those were the days before air conditioning. My dad was a *"jack of all trades;"* welder, mechanic, gardener, fisherman, and so on. People called Dad from all over with all kinds of requests.

"Hey, Sam, (my dad's name was Sam, too) *can you please come fix our washing machine? It stopped working."*

"I ran into a deer, and my car's all beat up. Can you fix it?"

"Our water pipe broke last night, and it needs to be dug up. Can you bring the backhoe right away?"

You name it; they asked my dad to fix it. He always found a way to fix even the stubbornest problem. Many a time, I heard a person say, "I never thought that could be fixed!" He was a "wanted" man; people recognized his talents and didn't mind using 'em.

I was talking with my dad shortly before he died. He was worried that he hadn't done enough for other people. He even requested that we sing *"Will There Be Any Stars in My Crown?"* at his funeral! As I'm writing this, I'm reminded of countless things my dad did for others. Looking back now, that's *all* he did. Isn't it funny that the people who do the most for others always think they haven't done anything? It's gotta be a heart condition called a *servant's heart*.

In the spring, Dad would go to several people's farms and plant their massive gardens. He had a little Farmall Model-A garden tractor with all the attachments. He would till the plot, tend the garden, hill the potatoes, and irrigate the garden in the spring. In the fall, he would dig the produce out of the ground.

One year, he did a large garden for a particular neighbor, and after working there for a day or two, he said to me, "They didn't even say thank you."

I've thought a lot about this, and that's why I purposely try to thank people heartily for all they do for me. There are so many things I don't take for granted, like my health, my wife, my fingers, my children, my job, my house, the dog, the cat, running water…I could go on and on! I really, truly believe in the spirit of gratefulness, and it's hard for me to tolerate folks who think they deserve so much more than they have.

"Thanks never fed the dog," Dad would chuckle when someone remembered to thank him. It was his type of humor. I remember another thing he'd say when someone was bragging about themselves. "Talk is cheap. Whiskey costs money. Hahaha!"

Anyway, back to my story. Highway 52 ran right through the middle of our farm, and many local businesses would often use "Highway 52" as part of their official business name (e.g., Highway 52 Feeders). We'll revisit this later.

All of us farm kids started out in the public-school system. I was in grade seven when my Uncle Frank started the process of getting a private school system going for southern Alberta. Our public-school trustees did not take kindly to us all leaving and starting a private school. After all, there were thirty-six of us! So, they subpoenaed all our parents to the courtroom. But these guys didn't know my Uncle Frank! He wasn't afraid of any of them, or even their whole town altogether. When he believed in something, he just did it. He was their match in every way. I've lived with my wife for thirty-seven years, and every time I get going on a project energetically, she says I'm just like my Uncle Frank!

There was a certain fellow in the public-school system, Mr. Jefferson, who was the instigator of this court case. I remember the constant thin, tight smile that stayed on his mouth and never spread to his eyes. He had only one arm, but that didn't stop him from being very aggressive. How do I know this dude was aggressive? He was the assistant principal at the school I had attended for six years, and many a time I stood facing him in his office, wondering how hard the whipping was gonna be.

This might be foreign to some of you, but we got whipped many times in the public school. The most painful experience was when a solid pointer about four feet long was used on the back of our legs. This hurt like the devil! Some of my most unfortunate classmates, who happened to be poor at spelling, were marched around the entire classroom. Every time they failed to spell a word right, the teacher laid into the back of their legs with the pointer. Talk about humiliation. I can still vividly picture those poor kids getting whacked all around the schoolroom while everybody else snickered. Nothing was politically correct back in those days. Mean buggers, weren't they?

A couple of days before the big court case, which by now involved people from all over Alberta, Mr. Jefferson happened to be driving through our place on Highway 52. We ran an open-grazing pig operation, and one of our old sows had found an escape route under the fence and wandered up on the highway just as he approached! My cronies and I were standing there visiting about 100 yards away, when I looked up and saw this old blue car heading straight for the poor sow, which was standing smack in the middle of the road.

Now, remember, this guy had only one hand to steer his car. *BOOM!* Mr. Jefferson hit that old sow at top speed and then put on a performance that ought to have been recorded in the *Guinness Book of World Records*. Mr. Jefferson could have taken the record for one-hand steering competition, hands down, no pun intended. I never saw a man use one hand in such a dramatic way. I thought for sure the car would roll, but it ended upright, just a few feet from us. Lo and behold, who stepped out of that old blue car but the very man who was intent on taking us to court! Well, well, life gets pretty strange at times!

In the Bible, I've read about a snake talking in a garden and another time a donkey talking to a prophet. It's funny how the snake in the garden of Eden changed the history of mankind and how the donkey changed the course of the mad prophet. Now, I saw with my own eyes how a tragic encounter with an old sow brought us face to face with a man trying to stop us from having our own school. This old sow totally changed the course of Mr. Jefferson's life, and she did this all by herself. He was not planning to stop by our place that evening for such an embarrassing moment. He could truly say that a pig had altered his destiny.

Presently, this fine gentleman who stepped out of the car told us we needed to keep our hogs penned up. We told him, "You sure did some mighty fine driving for a man with just one hand!" So now, instead of just taking us to court over the school issue, he has another serious grievance against us. We needed to keep our pigs secure behind their fence, and I totally agreed. If I remember right, the older people on the farm were a little bit scared of the repercussions of an old sow getting out on the road and being hit. What if Mr. Jefferson claimed some kind of permanent injury? My thought, being a young fellow at the time, was that the whole incident was pretty funny. Here a guy is taking us to court, and just before the court date, he hits an old sow, bringing him face to face with the people he's trying to indict.

It reminds me of Haman in the Bible, who feasted with the King and Queen Esther just before his tragic end (Esther 7). I was glad Mr. Jefferson wasn't physically hurt, but I didn't mind at all that he was really shook up. We gave him a ride back to town, and the tow truck came for his car.

The night before the court case was exhilarating for us youngsters because our parents told us not to get on the school bus the next morning. They said that if the police should come and try to round us up, we should hide in the wheat field or in one of the hundreds of other splendid hiding places around the farm. So, come morning, I just saddled up my faithful horse, Smoky, and was many miles away before the school bus ever stopped at the corner.

Every one of our parents were in the courtroom that fateful morning. Mr. Jefferson, complete with his smug expression, strolled to the front of the tension-filled room. I didn't know if he was still shaking from hitting the old sow or how he was doing, but he got up in front of the courtroom and said to our parents, "Where are your children? Why are they not in school?"

If our parents had answered that we were in school, he would have said, "Your school is not recognized in Canada." An arrogant man, he made no effort to hide the cocky grin on his face.

The judge looked at him and said, "Mr. Jefferson, before you start questioning these folks, I need to see your subpoenas for the children."

Mr. Jefferson opened up a suitcase and started rustling through his papers. He fumbled on for a few minutes, then looked up at the judge, his face turning pale. "I seem to have forgotten them, Your Honor," he stammered.

The judge took his gavel, slammed the desk, and declared, "This is an act of God!" He looked at our parents, who were sitting sort of dazed-like. "Ladies and gentlemen," he boomed, "You have your school! Court dismissed!"

I think that's the last time I ever saw Mr. Jefferson! He's been out of sight and out of mind for about forty years. I like it when things work out that way...*Yeah, Yeah, Baby!* We now had our own school, but that's another story.

Now you know how an old sow helped start private schools in windy southern Alberta. Many times in my life, people have asked me how I know the Bible is true. After all, the scribes that God used to write the Old and New Testament were very wicked people at some time in their lives! Whether they were or not, it doesn't make much difference to me. I've seen God use an old sow to accomplish His work, so I'm sure He has no problem using wicked men to accomplish His purpose. God can even use wicked people as instruments for a good outcome.

THE TEMPTATION TO GET BENT OUT OF SHAPE

It was Memorial Day weekend. We had just worked all day long, packing our old U-Haul truck with all our earthly possessions. We drove all night towards Fort Worth, Texas from northern Michigan. Around five o'clock the next morning, I started to see double, so I decided to pull over to get a couple of hours of sleep.

As I laid down on the seat, I notice an ominous cloud of smoke billowing up from under the hood of the old U-Haul. I quickly ran up front to see an injector line with a small crack spraying diesel fuel all over a smoking hot engine. I wrapped a rag around the leaking line as quickly as I could. When I was positive there was no danger of fire, I tried to get a few hours of rest across the pickup seat. The outside temperature read above 100° Fahrenheit.

Did I explain why I was pushing so hard to make it to Fort Worth? In the back of the truck was a large deep freezer full of food that we desperately did not want to thaw and spoil.

My first temptation was to get all down and discouraged and start singing the blues. Instead, I decided it was time to start praising God and believe there was a reason for this to be happening. I started mentally reciting Romans 8:28 over and over, telling myself that all things work together for good. But my reasoning, rational mind kept telling me that God had a lot bigger fish to fry on this holiday weekend than to help me find a fuel line, especially on a day where all the stores were closed and where I didn't know a living soul.

Much to my dismay, I discovered that the broken line was not one that runs along the engine's topside, but the seemingly impossible one at the very bottom of all the lines, meaning that all the other lines would have to come off first to get at this one.

After working for an hour in the 100° Texas weather on a 150° engine, we finally managed to get the broken line free using wrenches that a real mechanic wouldn't even think of to remove injector lines on a 7.3-liter diesel. With my hands all greasy and several fingers bleeding, but a big smile on my face, I look around to see an older couple getting ready to pull out of the rest area. I ask if I could get a ride into the next town. They looked me over good, and when I mentioned that I would ride in the back of their S-10, they agreed. They then drove me eight miles in the wrong direction, but because there was a gas station at the intersection, I jumped off the truck and went inside.

A young lady at the counter overheard me say I needed a ride back the other way and offered to give me a lift. I told her, "I'm a Christian; you have nothing to fear."

"I'm not afraid of you at all," she said. As we jumped into her car, I realized why she was so fearless! There was a monster pit bull, probably named Killer, in the back seat! He immediately put his huge, ugly head two inches from one of my big ears. She had to keep telling him to behave the whole way.

My two main thoughts the next 10 miles were, *"I wonder what it would feel like to lose an ear,"* and, *"I hope this dog obeys better than some kids I know."* Still just inches from my ear, Killer was drooling on my shoulder, slobbering like he was just getting ready for supper or something. Boy, am I glad when we reached our destination and I bid them both good-bye!

She dropped me off at an O'Reilly Auto Parts store that happened to be open on the Sunday of Memorial Day weekend. They took one look at the fuel line and informed me that it was a high-pressure line and because only Ford Motors Company carries it, I would have to wait two days for it.

Oh, brother! Trust me, it took a very conscious effort to keep praising God at this time, especially with a thousand dollars' worth of food thawing in the back of my ancient U-Haul. We remembered the last time things seemed impossible, we just started praising God, even though we had no clue how things would work out, and they did. So here we were again, in another impossible situation, looking at a two-day wait with a freezer full of food.

So, what did I do? I gave God the freezer full of food. It's kind of ironic how, when I'm in control, everything is mine, but the minute I'm about to lose it, I quickly give it to God. As we milled around the store, not knowing what to do next, I said, "God, I just praise You all the more…yes, Praise the Lord anyway! Determined not to cuss or become discouraged, I asked again, "Is there no one you know who might be able to help me?" But the answer was still negative.

I milled around the store a little more, and just as I was about to walk out the door, a big fellow approached me and said, "Maybe I can help you. I overheard your conversation, and I know a man who has a 7.3 diesel sitting outside his shop. If you want to come with me, I'll take you there." I did just that, and when I asked him what he did for a living, he informed me that he was a bouncer at a bar and had been beaten nearly to death by a group of thugs a couple of weeks prior. He had just been released from the hospital after some major surgeries.

"Do you wonder why that happened?" I asked him.

He explained, "I was trying to be a good guy and do what was right, but I was just at the wrong place at the wrong time."

"May I get a little personal?" I inquired of him.

"Fire away," was his response.

"What's your definition of good?" I began.

"Well, do unto others as you would have them do to you."

Then I asked if he felt that he was good enough to go to Heaven or satisfy God. "I hope the good outweighs the bad," he answered.

"Do you know why the Ten Commandments were given?"

"No," he said.

"Ever lied?"

"Lots of times."

"Ever lusted after the opposite sex?"

"All the time."

"Then, by your admission, you're a lying, thieving adulterer at heart."

"I see," he said finally.

"Does that bother you? Do you want to meet God that way?" I probed.

He studied me for a moment and said, "You know why your truck broke down? So, I could meet you. I needed to hear this."

That opened the door for me to share the good news of salvation to which he listened eagerly, asking a few questions now and then. Before long, we pulled into a field where a friend of his had an old 7.3 diesel sitting in the high grass. By the grace of God, the injector line that we needed was still on it.

The owner only wanted $7.00 for it, but I was so grateful that I handed him a twenty. We jumped into my new friend's car once more, drove to the closest gas station, and filled his car with fuel as a personal "thank you." He then hauled me over to my truck, where we parted as new friends.

Ten minutes later, I was roaring down the highway, rejoicing that I hadn't become discouraged. Rejoicing, too, that God cared enough about a bouncer at a bar to soften his heart so he would be open to the good news of salvation. I also rejoiced for my new-found bouncer friend.

I wondered about all the opportunities I may have blown during the many times I've gotten angry and cursed, and didn't believe that all things work together for those who know their God. It has been a comfort to me that God always knows where my lost possessions are and that He never tires of me asking Him to help me find them. What an awesome Friend He is! He loves at all times! And by the way, God never let His food spoil!

My son-in-law had his truck stolen with all his tools in it. It was gone for a month or more, and then one day, he phoned me and kind of discouragingly asked, "What can I do? I'm driving on to my big job-sites in a little old Honda car, and that's not too good an image for a builder in a big city." I asked him if he praised the Lord for the little Honda and everything that was happening, and he promised me that he would do just that.

The very next day, he phoned me, "You're never going to believe this!" he exclaimed, "After a month, the police found my truck and all my tools, and it's all in good shape!"

"Hello-o-o-o?" as Pooh Bear would say, *"hello-o-o-o?"*

MY GOD, THERE'S A LOT OF BENS

Way, way back when I was just a young man (though it seems like yesterday and most of my dreams are still from that era), I lived in windy southern Alberta on a vast farm/ranch that was spread out over a 100-mile radius. Our home farm consisted of 3,800 acres where five families lived within about a quarter-mile from each other.

Everywhere I go, I meet lonely people who are trying to find some kind of fellowship. But, back on the ranch, if you wanted to have some fun or if you just wanted to hang out, there was always a willing and ready cousin not too far away. Living close together with a group of people you see every day has its pros and cons, but I'd definitely say it has more pros if the people you're living with are half-decent human beings. I lived there 'til my late twenties and experienced many good, some bad, and still fewer ugly things, but I choose to focus on all the good memories.

For instance, in winter, we'd try to have a minimum of one hockey game a week. Everybody showed up on hockey night. The neighbors, all the cousins, the old folks, and some of the ladies would come out, even if it were 30° to 40° below zero. Many times, I remember having my toes so frozen that I couldn't feel them. In fact, the hockey games were much better attended than the Wednesday night prayer meetings. I remember that a lot of folks didn't worship in the same church and separated over the stupidest things, but when it came to hockey, everyone showed up with their differences left behind.

Springtime was spent working long grueling hours, tilling and seeding the ground, taking care of the range cattle, and just doing what needed to be done. Summertime was spent swimming, fishing, going back to the mountains for camping trips, playing baseball, and just having a good time. Then came the fall, and harvest time, which made everyone forget the clock and work like beavers.

We would start combining in the morning as soon as the grain was ripe, and work late into the night. If there was no dew, we would work 'til one or two o'clock in the morning. The harvest had to be brought in before we could play. Nobody I knew had a nine to five job; that was unheard of. A man just had to do what a man had to do.

One memory I have is the night my one uncle was playing goalie at our hockey game without wearing any protection for his procreating tools. One of the players took a slap shot on him, connecting right below his belt buckle and really hurting him. You would think a person would have a little common sense when someone wasn't wearing proper goalie protection, but no, that would be sane! He had to pretend he was Gordy Howe or Wayne Gretzky or somebody like that in the big leagues.

Well, the game went on for a little while, and this guy skated past Uncle again with a dumb grin on his face, went behind Uncle, then put his stick between his legs and tripped him. This dude was always picking a fight or trying to get other people to fight, so this behavior was pretty typical for him. Next thing, I saw both of them on the ground, fighting and carrying on like a couple of tomcats or two roosters fighting for dominance.

This particular young man was always bragging about how tough he was - how he could fight two men at once. On this bitter winter night, I'm sure he thought that he was stronger than my aging uncle! But when Uncle got ahold of this man jewels and started squeezing hard as he could, all the fight left Mr. Toughie! He began to wail and 'beller' and carry on so hard, you would have thought he was having a baby! To me, he sounded like a raging bull smelling blood! It made a big impression on me, because my inquisitive, imaginative brain never forgot how bad that must have hurt!

We had horses, hogs, chickens and a big feedlot on the home farm, plus all the equipment, shops, and buildings you needed to operate. In addition to the home farm, about fifty miles to the east, we farmed another twelve sections called the Henninger Ranch. Then fifty miles to the west of us was the Blood Indian Reservation, where we leased around 8,500 acres, right near the tall shadows of the Rocky Mountains. This story took place in the small town of Spring Coulee, just a few miles off the reserve, which consisted of a few grain elevators, maybe twenty houses, and a tiny little grocery store.

Three of my uncles, who were not part of our immediate farm, also leased large farmland sections on the same reservation. With his three sons and a couple of sons-in-law, one of them had the largest farming operation of the bunch and was by far the most successful of the three.

Long before the day of the smartphone, we all owned two-way radios, which were necessary running three different farming operations. Everybody had their nickname and communicated with each other on the same channel. Having the radios kept us all in touch in case of a fire (which happened quite often), if someone needed help real fast, needed to know where the police set up their radar traps, where the lunch truck was, or if someone had a good story to tell. They came in very handy many a time.

My uncle happened to acquire a little more of this world's goods than some of the others. His family had the nicest vehicles, the latest in big trucks, the best tractors, and basically the best of everything. His kids would come to school with one-hundred-dollar bills in their pockets, while the rest of us were given a quarter on a good day, a dime on an average day, and a nickel on a sad day. Back in those days, a quarter bought a Coke, an O-Henry bar, a bag of chips, a pack of gum, and a handful of Mojos.

This uncle of mine, who had a little more than the rest of us, also had a son named Ben. I was a little younger than Cousin Ben and grew up wearing all his hand-me-down clothes. Looking back, life was very good because we were all taught to work hard, we were given lots of responsibility, and learned a lot about life.

For instance, I would get up around 5:00 A.M. to rush about a quarter-mile down the road during winter, summer, spring, and fall, to start my many chores. It took 120, five-gallon pails of rolled barley to satisfy the feedlot cattle. I'd run into the wooden feed shed, fill my buckets, then carry them 200 feet to the far end of the trough, and work my way back to the other end where the trough began. I remember feeling like a really big guy when I could finally muster the strength to carry four pails at a time. From there, I would go feed a bunch of hogs, rush home, clean up, eat some breakfast, grab my lunch pail, and head out to the big yellow school bus a quarter-mile south of our house.

Getting on the bus, I'd look around and see the other kids wipe the sleep from their eyes, still just trying to wake up. I remember thinking, *"Why do I have to work like this, and these other kids don't?"* But there were perks that came with it! Pitching bales, carrying feed, and lots of shoveling grain makes a body tough and strong. In grade seven, I was laying a whipping on the kids in grade twelve, out behind the old school, fighting with our bare fists. (I know I'm bragging here.)

My teacher in grade six was a man named Mr. Wood. One fine day he asked me in front of the whole class if I thought I was tough and if I'd arm wrestle him. I remember walking up front and beating him in both arms!! He was extra quiet the rest of the day and didn't appreciate all the snickers from the rest of the kids. On my fourteenth birthday, I was bench pressing 310 pounds, and at nineteen, I won the southern Alberta weight-lifting competition by curling 240 pounds! The prize given by 1090 Check, the local radio station, was a nice Bulova wristwatch. So, I took the watch and traded it for a ladies' watch with a diamond inlay, and gave it to the sweetest girl in all the world. Ahhhh!

I'm simply saying, we were taught to work. And I've never regretted it, because the things I learned back then have helped me out a million times since. I picture life like this; everything that happens to us, whether it's good or bad, and everything we learn to do or not do, is what I call our toolbox. For the rest of our lifetime, we use tools from our past, and we get new tools as we go into our future. Some people's toolbox has hardly anything in it, while other people's toolbox is full and running over.

Now back to the small town of Spring Coulee! We would drive past Spring Coulee on the way to the reservation and on the way back. The town was located where the bumpy, dusty, gravel road quit, and the nice smooth highway started. It was just perfect for picking up some grub from the quaint little country store and enjoying a nice, smooth ride home for the rest of the trip. Maybe it's just me, but I believe that things taste a lot better when you're not bouncing and up and down on a rough, dusty, gravel road.

My rich uncle, who had a little bit more of this world's goods than the rest of us, had a charge account set up at this quaint little country store. Sometimes, us young people had a bit of money, but most of the time we didn't. This was no big deal because, in our community, everyone knew everyone else, and there was a charge account in every store. Well, I remember how the boss, or should I say bookkeeper, on our farm told us we were charging way too much junk food on the farm's account. Well, well, well, I guess it's just the way a mind works because my mind immediately started to reason with itself. It told me our ranch might be low on funds, and things may be very, very, tight, but I did have one uncle who seemed to be thriving. Being as we were all closely related, I was sure my rich uncle wouldn't mind feeding a hungry nephew now and then since I did do a lot of chores for him.

I remember late one evening, I pulled up to the little store. I was terribly thirsty and hungry and didn't have a dime, but I grabbed everything off the shelf that I wanted, got myself a soda, and piled everything up on the counter. This little old lady said, "Five-seventy-five, please."

"Charge it," I said.

"To whose account please?" she inquired. I gave her my rich uncle's name.

"May I ask your name please?" At that point, I never looked up. I just said, "Ben." She then asked me to sign the piece of paper, so I scrawled some fancy signature that hopefully might look like Ben's, and that's when I heard her mutter under her breath, "My God, there's a lot of Bens!"

It was then revealed to me and helped soothe my tender conscience that without a shadow of a doubt, I was not the sole perpetrator guilty of using Uncle's account to fill my belly. Indeed, I was one of many relatives who had conveniently changed their name to Ben for a moment when hunger overtook the body, and it simply needed to be done.

JOJO'S BLACK STALLIONS

My sweetheart and I have been married since 1980, and we have been blessed with the pleasure and joy of having four incredible children—three girls and a boy.

As I grew up in windy southern Alberta, Canada, on a large farm/ranch, we had lots of horses to ride and to work with. So, when we got married, I was still very much involved with horses, and our children grew up watching me train them. Our two oldest daughters each owned a saddle horse, and I promised our youngest daughter, JoJo, that I would get her one, too.

They say there are always two sides to every story, so here's my perspective on how things unfolded; and, there's JoJo's perspective. They're both true. One evening I told her that I was leaving the next morning with the horse trailer to pick up a horse for her, one that she could name and call her very own. She was ecstatic! She probably didn't sleep much that night, and she probably envisioned a steed, like in the movie *The Black Stallion,* which she had watched often. All she could say was, "Thank you! Thank you! Thank you, Daddy!" It was my honest and only intent to find her a horse of her very own on that memorable day! That was my mission; get a beautiful horse for my little Jojo.

My friend Bill raised Arabian horses and a host of other animals for a living, and he even had his own pet monkey, who lived in the house with his family. Bill and I had done a lot of horse dealing and equipment trading through the years, and I had bought many a horse from him.

SON OF A SEACOOK

I was really low on cash at the time, and I had phoned Bill the day before and told him I had a slightly used Milwaukee Chop Saw that I could probably do without, and I wondered if he would be willing to do some horse-trading with me. Back then, we'd barter over everything and almost anything! You would never consider yourself broke if you had a piece of equipment kicking around your yard that you were not currently using. I remember one time I had a couple of guns that I had not used for a great while and traded Bill for two horses, or should I say two hay-burners. A hay-burner is what we'd call any horse that wasn't being used, or that wasn't quite broke yet.

JoJo's Black Stallion - What JoJo thought she was getting.

Our little girl was up bright and early the next morning, and excitedly bade me farewell and reminded me to hurry back as fast as I could. I drove the hour it took to get to Bill's animal farm and caught him just coming out of the house on his way to the barn. I shut off my truck and stepped out, hoping to hear something like this, "Hello, Sam! It sure is good to see you, Ol' Buddy!" or maybe "Man-o-man, you're looking good! Life must be treating you fine!" or even "How's that beautiful wife of yours? And the children?"

But Bill barely even glanced at me. "Where's that old Milwaukee saw of yours? Are you sure it's any good? You said only slightly used. Well, what about these scratches? And the blade looks pretty dull to me!"

I immediately sensed his frame of mind. Maybe his wife refused his advances and served him a cold breakfast, or perhaps his pet monkey crapped all over the floor again and tore up the house because he figured out how to escape his cage? Or maybe he just stepped out of the wrong side of the bed and didn't have time to collect his thoughts.

By his greeting, I knew from past experience that he was gonna try to drive a hard, hard bargain. Instantly I put on my "wise-as-a-serpent" mentality and causally suggested, "Maybe I shouldn't get rid of that saw after all. I just thought of a few things I might need it for."

This statement would increase my buying powers to make it seem as though I wasn't too hungry for a deal. I wanted Bill to think I just might drive back home with my Milwaukee cut off saw and my empty horse trailer. So now, after we both had set the stage for our little game of trading poker, we both figured we were in the best spot to swing a decent deal. He took another close look at my just-like-new, slightly used, Milwaukie chop saw, mumbled something under his breath, and told me to go pick out any two-year-old from his horse herd. Then maybe he would think about a good deal.

I was about to pick out a stunning black, two-year-old gelding, probably the best two-year-old in the herd, when Bill noticed and quickly climbed the fence where I was perched. "I have these two Jerusalem donkeys," he said eagerly, "Bee-uuu-ti-ful animals they are, and I'll trade you for the same amount as that black two-year-old!"

Well, I had never had anything to do with a donkey before, but I had heard that they were really good at keeping coyotes away from sheep. And hadn't Jesus rode on a borrowed one? I had never owned a donkey, had never heard a donkey bray, and hadn't the faintest clue what a powerful, awful sound they could make! I had never been within 100 feet of a donkey, and the main thing I heard about them was how stubborn they were.

Now, old Mr. Bill was quite the salesman, and I must say he was very smooth! His magic started to kick in as he walked up to the first donkey and started scratching it under the chin. The second donkey walked up friendly as all get out, so Bill scratched both donkeys simultaneously under their chin and across their backs, calm as could be. "Would you just step over here for a minute and look at this perfect cross on their backs?" he inquired of me. "It resembles the cross that our Lord Jesus died on! Look, Sam! These are Jerusalem donkeys because they have a perfect cross, and that's why our Savior rode on one."

"Wow!" I exclaimed, "Just wow!"

"And just maybe the cross appeared after our Lord dismounted?" He continued earnestly. "Maybe that's exactly what happened."

They say you can make a mistake once, and you're really not to blame, but if you make the same mistake twice, you have yourself to blame. I think that is very true.

I forgot all about the value of my just-like-new Milwaukee saw. I forgot all about the perfect little black gelding. I forgot all about my wise-as-a-serpent mentality. All I could think was that these have got to be two of the cutest, most unique animals I would ever have the opportunity to own, and my JoJo would love them! She would have something the two older girls didn't have, and better yet, she would own *two* of them!

Things started to get emotional, and we were both almost in tears as the sales web was being spun around my heart. My tears betrayed genuine emotion and sprang from a heart of love and the extraordinary Jesus story that had just been revealed to me.

My friend, Bill? I think his tears came from the idea that he'd never met a bigger fool than his friend Sam, and also from the joy of how easy it was to get rid of two spoiled, useless donkeys that were burning up his hay.

It was all over! I was so mesmerized and spiritualized that I forgot to think about my little seven-year-old daughter, her anticipation, and the sleepless night she must've had just thinking about her very own beautiful black stallion.

I thought it was a no-brainer, getting two-for-one, so just like that, we made a deal and got them loaded up in the back of the horse trailer before anyone could do any more swindling.

In retrospect, I should have thought more about my promises to JoJo and her feelings, and not so much about making a good money deal for myself or how cute those donkeys were. I pulled into our yard with a horse trailer and the two grey Jerusalem donkeys, just in time to see her come running from the house as fast as her little legs would carry her. She followed me till I brought the rig to a stop.

"Daddy! Daddy, did you get me a horse? Did you really get me a horse?" She yelled at the top of her lungs. Her eyes shone like two bright blue stars.

Dear reader, please forgive me. Forgive me for breaking that little lamb's heart! I was planning to bring her home a horse and very soon! Before she could see into the trailer and before I could act, both donkeys started braying and crying wildly, a sound none of us were used to. It sounded like the last day on the planet with the sky about to fall. JoJo looked at me with alarm written across her little face.

"Daddy! That doesn't sound like our other horses!"

I said, "Listen, Angel. You're going to love what I brought home for you. I didn't just get you one! I got you two!"

At this point came the sinking realization of the disappointment my little girl might experience when she saw my incredible bargain. Slowly, I opened the back door of that horse trailer, and my beautiful daughter just stood there and stared at the two startled Jerusalem donkeys who stood staring back at us.

JoJo's Black Stallion - What JoJo actually got!

"Daddy!" She said tearfully, "Them are donkeys! I don't *want* donkeys! I wanted a real *horse*, a big black one like Jess and Jackie!"

It was at this point that I knew I needed to move fast. I tried to tell JoJo how the deal had all come down and that I could make a quick buck and that I would get her a horse as soon as possible. My beautiful little JoJo didn't hear or understand any of my reasoning that day. All she understood in her childlike mind was that Dad had let her down! "My Daddy let me down! He promised me a horse and brought home two stupid donkeys instead!"

I had shattered her expectations. Done. I've never forgotten that day. It helped me remember that every time I talk to a youngster, I need to be super careful about what I promise them, even down to saying, "We'll go fishing soon," or, "I'll take you for ice cream," or anything else.

I currently have two sets of twin grandchildren. I went fishing the other day with the two five-year-old girls. The three of us got in the boat and paddled out to the middle of the lake. "Grandpa's gonna catch a big fish today…just watch him," I bragged.

One of them piped up and said, "Grandpa, you can't say that because you don't know if you'll catch one. You can only say you hope you catch a fish." Not bad thinking for a little five-year-old! I often say something to them and hear about it two or three days later. Very young children are tuned in to everything you're saying, just like the Pentagon's best high-tech spying equipment.

Now, back to my little JoJo. The story indeed does have a happy ending because we got her a couple of nice horses later on. Many times in the last thirty years, she has reminded me of the Jerusalem donkeys and that fateful day when her expectations were shattered.

But I'm not finished with my donkey stories just yet.

Back in those years, I was actively involved in the local community and several different ministries. People were always coming and going from our yard because we tried connecting with everyone we could to try to show them the love of Jesus in a practical way. Southern Alberta has a substantial Mormon population. These folks are very evangelical, mission-minded, family-oriented, and are excellent neighbors. When they discovered that we were well-connected in the local community, they often asked me to join their church. One elder told me that if they didn't get me in this life, they would get me in the next one, but they would get me to join 'em! Well, at least I can say I was a wanted man.

On my little farm, I had a forty-by-sixty shop with the garage door facing east. That way, when the Chinook wind blew, it wouldn't affect my building because the robust and prevailing wind always came from the west. If you had a garage door facing west, in my humble opinion, your buildings would potentially lift off like a parachute, exponentially increased if you happened to have your garage door open. I've seen it happen several times where the Chinook wind grabbed massive buildings, and when they hit the ground, there was nothing left but rubble. I totally placed the blame on the direction that the openings in the buildings were facing. I'll just say this - if you wanna live in southern Alberta, then you better get used to the wind.

One day I was working in my shop and my neighbor, Zack, whom I did a lot of work for, happened to drop by. This gentleman was a Mormon bishop, so we would have lots of discussions concerning life and the hereafter. I would try to convert him to Christianity, and he tried to get me to join the Mormons. On each one of our many discussions, we'd both come up with our most convincing new angles of thought, trying to get the other to see things our way. On this particular day, I was standing in my big garage door, facing towards the east, and he was standing on the north side of my garage door, facing me. You may ask why this is important. It is imperative, trust me. Behind my bishop friend to the north were the corrals and the shelter where our two new donkeys resided.

Zack said to me, "Sam, I'd like to make you an offer."

"Okay, fire away. Pertaining to what?"

Then he said, "I've been watching how you and your wife live, and I'm very impressed because you live a whole lot better than a lot of our members do! I'm a temple cardholder, and I have the church's authority to make you an offer."

"Oh?" I inquired, kinda interested in what he had to say.

He said, "You and your wife could come to our temple in Cardston, where we would remove most of your earthly clothing and dress you in robes of white. Next, we would dedicate all your body parts to God to be used for time and eternity. I'll have to warn you, Sam, if you refuse this once-in-a-lifetime offer, you will be a sorry, sorry man!"

I thought to myself, "He sure has a lot to offer me - a massive, beautiful temple and all these religious rituals. What do I have to offer? Repent, believe in Jesus, and gain eternal life! How beautiful, how simple to have a direct connection to God with no priest, no temple, no rituals, just God and me.

"On the final day of judgment, I will be way above you horizontally," Zack continued. "Legally speaking, you can only go to the terrestrial level of Heaven if you don't join our church. But, if you accept our temple rituals, you can make it all the way through the terrestrial to the celestial and be right in the presence of God!"

He stepped closer and looked me right in the eye. "Wouldn't you want what's best for your wife? To be eternally married to her Sam?" he asked sincerely, his eyes glistening a bit. "Wouldn't you want to make celestial love to her throughout all eternity, be the only god on your very own star creating spirit babies so that earthlings can have spirits for the bodies that they're producing on Earth? That way, the earth can continue to be populated, and the cycle of life can continue! Wouldn't you?"

"Wait a minute!" I thought to myself. Instead, I replied, "My question is, how much higher will you be than me?" I still have the picture in my mind of my friend when he answered me.

He stretched out his hand towards the heavens and said, "I will be above you in the highest celestial heavens at about a 45° angle, and I will be creating my own worlds just like God!"

The part that intrigued me the most was the 45° angle. I was not sure how he figured the angle's geometry, but I knew the last thirty years I had been telling my sweetheart that she was so much better than I was when it came to sound, dedicated, practical, saintly living. I knew that on the last day, she would be way higher than me, likely in the direction of a 45° angle. Both of us see where the angle comes from!

My good bishop friend still had his hand in the air at about a 45° angle and was just finishing with the geometry lesson, when from behind him, from their lowly stables, both donkeys burst forth in a braying session! The sounds were so loud, so horrifyingly unmelodious that I'm sure the unsuspecting neighbors living two miles away heard them! There was an utter terror on poor Zack's face as he seemed to be lifting off the ground and rapidly closing the gap between himself and his celestial city. Then he did something that the engineers say is aerodynamically impossible! As he was at the peak of his flight, he did a one-eighty in midair, trying to find the source of that awful sound! All I heard was, "What the hell was that? I never knew you had donkeys - dumb buggers!"

I said, "My friend, I'm so sorry about the scare, but I just bought them yesterday."

Let me just wind up the story here. I spoke with my daughter the next day on the phone and told her what happened. She was able to shed some light on the reason my dear friend Zack was so jumpy. She told me how he had come on the farm one day when I wasn't home and that our big billy goat had gotten out of his pen and rammed into the back of Zack's legs, sending him sprawling to the ground. She said she was talking to Mr. Zack when it had happened and that she was utterly mortified at what our billy goat had done to a friend of ours.

She said, "Daddy, the billy just came out of nowhere, and I didn't even have time to scream or warn poor Zack. Luckily, I was there because the billy was trying to get him again as he got up off the ground. I knew we couldn't let that happen again!"

"It's alright, baby," I told her. "Zack will be fine, but now I know why he was so jumpy today. One more question."

"Yes, Daddy?"

"Did he mention anything about a 45° angle as he was getting off the ground?"

SON OF A SEACOOK

CON MAN

Someone once said to me, "You know, Sammy, if you ever stuck with anything, you could really make something of yourself." But it seems like a person can try a lot of different things and soon lose interest in them. Yes! Each endeavor may have succeeded if you would have stayed on course.

"Many thanks for your opinion," I thought to myself. *"But if you only knew my friend, that I would love to explore a thousand more avenues in this short life though I realize that time will never allow all my ideas to materialize!"*

So I'll endeavor to choose my priorities carefully, and the Lord willing, maybe we'll see more of my plans succeed! I've always dreaded living without a vision and becoming sloppy, careless, and stagnant in life, so I was all over the occupational map as a young man. I began as a farmer/rancher and then started my own construction business, which specialized in grain handling systems for big companies like Cargill, Alberta Wheat Pool, Pioneer Grain, and many others that operated along the Canadian rail lines.

My next venture included a welding and machine shop where we fabricated luxury pontoon boats and many other items made of steel. After that, I became an evangelist, salesman, musician, and songwriter. This sounds too much like bragging to suit me, so I'll stop right there.

Pontoon Boat

I'm writing this to make a point. When you are in business with many different folks, you get a hands-on education of getting to know people, and you learn to trust your gut more than anything they say. After a while, it's hard for some character to pull a fast one on you because this is not your first rodeo. So while I may not have stuck with one occupation for too long, I generally stick with my opinions or gut feelings about individuals and decide if I want to continue interacting with them or just get while the getting's good. I've always had a powerful sense of right and wrong and pretty sound intuition when it comes to figuring out what makes a person tick and how they think. Maybe another time, I'll describe our attempt to run a halfway house where we tried to help a bunch of freeloading con artists, but that's another story.

This intuition came in very handy one fall when my crew and I built a grain elevator in a small Alberta town several hours away. To avoid a long, daily commute, my family and I and most of our crew lived in a local campground for four months. My wife cooked for the whole crew while our young daughters ran around the campground, talking everyone's ears off.

One evening we decide to check out the mid-week Bible study in this small town, just to see what was happening and maybe make some new friends. After all, when it's just you and your crew for four months, you sometimes get a hankering for some more varied company.

We arrived at this quaint little country church, introduced ourselves, and told them that for the next four months we would be building a grain elevator right in town along the railroad tracks. Everyone was all smiles as they welcomed us heartily. All seemed well, and we were looking forward to more fellowship with these folks.

The service started and we all sat in a circle holding hands, which was entirely new for me. I was relieved that the people on either side of me were ladies because I didn't relish the thought of holding a man's hand through a long prayer. When the prayer ended, all the good, down-home, country-raised, beef-and-chicken-fed, trusting, hardworking, believing folks did their very best in worshipping our good Lord.

As the service came to a close, a lady sitting next to me started telling me of a certain Amish gentleman living in the local community who was usually part of their meetings. She told me how this gentleman could praise the Lord, play guitar, speak in tongues, and do a whole gamut of religious activities, and that we need to come back soon to meet him. It sounded like they had everything the church needed, all gift-wrapped in the form of one lone Amishman.

I've seen folks all over the eastern United States use the name "Amish" to sell their products and make money. I've seen Amish bread, Amish pie, Amish milk, Amish cheese, Amish geese, Amish beef, Amish furniture, Amish popcorn, Amish chicken, Amish quilting, and about ten-thousand other things with the word "Amish" attached to them. I've even seen ladies of the night pretending to be Amish and perform their services amongst the Plain People. I've seen all these things, but never have I seen an Amishman living all by himself on the bald prairies of southern Alberta, Canada, much less one that plays guitar and speaks in tongues.

"Hmmm," I started thinking, "so this is where Harrison Ford got the idea for the movie *"The Witness."* Things were starting to make sense. I was beginning to think that most of these *"English Gentiles"* didn't know much about the Amish culture, and what they did know was gathered from a movie.

English folks tend to view the Amish as they would view going to a zoo for an afternoon of entertainment. I suppose this is why they never thought it strange for an Amishman to live alone with no community or Amish church, on the wind-swept prairies of southern Alberta. I have quite the imagination so at this point I began to theorize just how this lone Amishman came to reside in this area. Maybe he had been part of a large migration of the Amish heading west and got left behind somehow. Maybe his buggy broke down irreparably. Perhaps he was at the back of the buggy train, and his horse meandered off while he was taking a nap. Maybe the other Amish didn't like the songs he played on his guitar and chose to desert him in the middle of the night. If the last scenario were true, that would mean this poor Amish gentleman was just like the Amalekite whose master left him to die after they had plundered King David's city of Ziklag (1 Sam. 30:1-18). In that case, I could feel a little sorry for him, but I began to highly doubt this conclusion when I remembered all the Amish people I had been in contact with. They live in a communities with a church and multiple families. They abstain from playing any instruments and use their voices to praise our good Lord. And they never, ever speak in tongues.

Since my imaginative mind was overly inquisitive, I dared to ask how it could be that an Amish gentleman was living alone on the prairies. As I said before, I know a bit about the Amish, and it sounded like this lone character was a fish out of water.

"Are you sure he's a genuine Amishman?" I asked.

"Oh yes!" said a little old lady. "He even has a hex sign on his barn."

I nodded as if I understood her reasoning, but I was thinking, "What on earth does a hex sign have to do with anything?"

"Oh! By the way," the lady added, "He gets treatments for Agent Orange in a hospital in Ohio, and our fellowship has given him seven-thousand dollars to pay for his plane tickets."

Uh oh! Red flag. Wait. *What?!* The second she mentioned all the cash involved there were alarm bells, flashing lights, and multiple sirens going off in my head. I had so many questions for these dear, sweet, loving country folks!

"In what city in Ohio is the hospital located?"

"What's the name of the hospital?"

"Has anyone called the hospital?"

"Has anyone verified that the fine gentleman was in Vietnam where Agent Orange was used?

"Are there any military records?"

I knew that Amish people aren't affiliated with the military. They live in communities, never alone. And very little you see in the movies is real or true to their lives.

So here I was, asking all kinds of questions about a man that they had given their church offerings to.

Initially, all I received from these dear, trusting country folks were "deer-in-the-headlights" stares, and I began to get a little discouraged thinking that they might not believe me. I had placed a few long distance phone calls and discovered that this speaking-in-tongues, guitar-playing dude was a con man who had already worn out his welcome in Holmes County, Ohio. Ya, those good folks knew the con man personally and now they had the buckets of hot tar and the goose feathers waiting in case he showed up one more time.

But wait!

Somethings a happening!

Suddenly it seemed as though the Spirit was moving around the room, as understanding slowly began to sweep through the small crowd of old people. It reminded me of a soft breeze blowing across a tall, ripe wheat field, making gentle ripples throughout the amber waves of grain. One by one, heads started bobbing in acknowledgment as the truth "pierced the veil." They all had this faraway look in their eyes, and many were stroking their chins, deep in thought, possibly recalling a previous experience with a swindler.

We all know that hindsight is 20/20, and these good folks were wondering now how on earth they had missed this con's game. A wave of disbelief swept over the crowd, rising at the pulpit and splashing off the back wall as some of the older, more experienced folks recalled the checks they got in their spirits when the con man gave his theatrical testimony. The elaborate, exaggerated, dramatic wickedness and overrated sorrow of his past. The tragic story of how he lost both parents in a fiery accident, when he was just barely 9 years old, and he had to look out for the rest of the family. (W*e later talked with them, and they were very much alive*). How he bravely fought through the hordes of hell just to get to this little country church in the middle of nowhere.

As I continued observing, more than one person looked a bit green around the gills and several of them appeared to be giving themselves a mental shake.

Why had they ignored their gut instinct?

How on earth had they allowed themselves to be so deceived?

I believe the peer pressure of that emotionally charged moment had overridden their good sense of judgment. The general congregation aside, let's focus on the emotions of those that wrote the checks to our dear Amish con man. While everyone else was experiencing feelings of slight consternation, the poor deacon was absolutely freakin'. You see, he was the church treasurer, and it was beginning to dawn on him how many years it took to collect this amount of money into his coffers. He quickly snatched up his solar-powered calculator and started to do some figuring of his own.

You see, this little country church wasn't like some of the mega-churches of the 2000's. They couldn't raise $20,000.00 for a guest evangelist! No way, Jose! They probably couldn't raise that amount in a decade, and here they had blindly given it all to a traveling con man. Yup!

This church had no youth among them so it was more of an old folks' social hangout. If the preacher did his utmost best (which didn't often happen because his salary was the same regardless) the money would start to trickle in by dimes, nickels, a stray bolt washer, a few quarters, or maybe on a good day a whole dollar. Otherwise folks mainly came to the meetings for a good nap, a potluck dinner, a few friendly jokes, and the latest gossip. They suffered in silence as the small-town pastor rattled on and on, so intrigued by the sound of his own voice that he seldom realized no-one was listening.

Now here they were, with the realization settling in that they had given all this money to a perfect stranger, and suddenly they began to think about the many ways that money could have been effectively spent. It could have helped Uncle Hank with the meds he could no longer afford; dear old sister Anna who needed funds for her cancer treatment, poor crippled Mary with the new wheelchair lift she needed so badly to get into her van, Mary's husband John, who had arthritis so bad he couldn't milk the cows and couldn't afford the 300 dollar repair for the air pump to run the milkers, or even Aunt Molly who was so obese that she either needed her stomach sewed shut or the new liposuction operation she had spied in the big city newspaper. Not to mention the carpet in the aisle of the church was still the original carpet from 1902 and desperately needed to be replaced.

The situation was even starting to upset me! I saw many dire needs and how people were struggling and some old geezer gave the church money away to someone he didn't even know. That really stung the congregation. They went on to find another treasurer and kind of ostracized the old one. When I called the pastor a few weeks later he said they were all going after the con man to get their money back (It never happened).

I like how another minister from a different church and a different situation put it. He said "Please don't bring your money and give it to this church because I work a good job, and I have enough. The old wood stove in the back of the church burns a few logs throughout the year which aren't hard to get. If you want to give money, go find someone whose groceries you can buy or whose husband has left them, and take care of the needs in your community."

Amen to that!

It's incredible how intense an emotional attachment the little church had formed to the con man. Despite the support I was getting from some of the congregation, others still believed in the con man's message! He had several little old ladies wrapped around his slippery fingers. They sat there in their pews, shaking their feeble heads back and forth and glaring at me like I was the devil himself, trying to destroy a poor Amish brother.

After dismissal one morning, several of the ladies reiterated how he could praise the Lord. The incident reminded me of Mark Twain's "Huckleberry Finn." I think Old Mark Twain experienced something first hand to be able to write about the king and the duke fleecing the entire town. This was probably the playbook for this wandering fellow.

I was very suspicious of this Amish dude and I set out to prove my hunch to the congregation. So myself and two of my brothers-in-law who were on my crew determined to find this exceptional man of God...this wonder of the 20th century...this revolutionary legend who had his roots in the Amish community.

One evening after work, we made the trip out to his farm. Sure enough, right in the middle of a Gentile community on the prairies of Alberta was a real live Amishman! It was a frigid, blustery day, and I happened to be wearing a beaver skin hat like the Royal Canadian Mounted Police wear.

A short, powerfully built man opened the door to our knock, glanced at my hat and started fidgeting nervously. First this way, then that, this way, then that, acting like a cornered coyote, with this sickening expression on his face.

"Good grief," I thought, "this man acts like he just met a bunch of federal agents, or like a youngster getting caught with his hand in the forbidden cookie jar."

Feeling the heavy tension of the situation and wanting to defuse it, I quickly said, "Praise the Lord!" and watched the amazing transformation as the chameleon turned colors right in front of us. Gone was the look of guilt and anxiety. Gone was the dark, drawn countenance. Immediately, a synthetic, sanctimonious holiness took its place. That face before us was transformed in a microsecond to the look of a fox that had just been let into the hen house. He even dropped his voice to a lower decimal and added a little waver and tremble to it, thereby adding sound effects to his façade of holiness.

At any rate, when our new friend heard "Praise the Lord!" it's like we flipped his Jesus switch into high gear. We were invited into his dwelling and seated so we had the privilege to face his collection of religious study books. At the same time, he proceeded to "bear testimony," as my old Mormon neighbors would have put it. He was not fooling me, but it wasn't for lack of trying or skill. You see, this fine fellow didn't have to try to con anyone because he is a con. It's like the late Buck Owens said, *"All I gotta do is act naturally."* His inner man, his internal hard drive, his modus operandi, were all programmed to con, con, con.

Now, with the three of us sitting in front of him, he was going through his routine with remarkable skill. It was as if he couldn't believe his good fortune; that he had a golden opportunity to hone his persuasive skills further and sharpen his wits. Usually a man must hunt to find his game, or in this instance, go to a church to find gullible prey, but we spared this guy the effort!

It reminded me of one day when I was preparing to go hunting. I packed my lunch, got my warm clothes, assembled all my hunting gear, and took the whole evening to get ready for a few days' hunting the surrounding hills for a big buck. I stepped outside the door of my house, and right there in my field stood a nice, big, beautiful buck that seemed to be saying, "Shoot me!" So I did. It doesn't get much better than that.

So, like that buck and I, the con man's prey came right to him. Except he hadn't gone to the trouble of packing his gear or anything. I'm sure he was thinking something along the lines of, "It's a good day in the neighborhood. Three uninvited fools show up of their own free will, right at my doorstep to be fleeced and robbed."

So after being entirely convinced that us three sheep were ready for the shearing and that the noose of deception was fitted tightly around our unsuspecting necks, he gave us the longwinded, tragic testimony that won over the gullible church sheeple. I've got to give this guy some credit here; I don't think I have ever seen another class of acting on this level. It was sheer genius. The dude was very smooth, to say the least. I quickly glanced at my two brethren only to see them wiping their brimming eyes, somewhat like you would if you were watching "Secretariat" for the very first time. Now comes the fatal moment in which I realized that I was standing alone. I was the only truth standing between the fleecier and those about to be fleeced. Just as a cat would crouch and slowly inch towards the unsuspecting mouse, the swindler went to the bookshelf and pulled out a little book. This book was all about why a man should join the plain Amish style of life and why people should dress and act like the early Quakers at the turn of the century.

I happened to know that the fellow who wrote this book was a professional con artist as well, so pulling out the book was another strike against our little Amish con man as far as I was concerned. But, people as a whole were blinded to the author's faults because he knew how to say all the right words, and all they could see was his long beard, plain clothes, suspenders, and black hat. With his reading material notwithstanding, the demonstration was totally professional. The verses that he shared from his Bible were all underlined, and big crocodile tears hit the page as he unremittingly continued. He said his father had died as an alcoholic, and his mother perished some other dreadful way. I could hear the gasps of sensation from my two brothers-in-law, who are trying to keep their tears from spilling over. When the chap could see how taken in the brothers were, he ramped up his act once more, like a fighter pilot engaging the afterburners on his F-14 Tomcat. Isn't it crazy how a little bit of affirmation will make a storyteller double down and try to get another "wow" out of a person?

Many years ago, a group of us fellows traveled to Los Angeles to see the big city's sights and sounds and reach out to the homeless. Each night after we were done with the day's activities, we gathered at the hotel for testimony and prayer time. Some of the young fellows slipped into a competition mode, as young men tend to do, to see who could give the best testimony. Each night the testimonies got bigger, better, bolder, and longer, with increasing trauma described each time they were eagerly given.

One young fellow, who had scarcely seen twenty seasons come and go, began his testimony by saying he used to drink a case of beer and do a 100 dollars' worth of drugs a day. I quickly did a little mental calculation and figured he'd have to have had a pretty decent job for such liberal indulgences, but it was still possible, and maybe I was too quick to bring a judgment call against this great sinner. However, the past wickedness of this young entrepreneur of elaborate sinning leaped about a thousand percent, and by the end of the week, he claimed to have drunk a couple of cases of beer and used 800 dollars' worth of drugs each day.

I happened to know where the young fellow worked, so one night, I tried to reason with him that although his sins were very great, a job paying eight dollars an hour, even though the hands of a diligent housewife stretched it, could never sustain an 800 dollar-a-day habit. No, never, no matter how much she'd try. He saw the light and confessed he may have slightly overdramatized and entered into the spirit of competition a little too much.

And that's precisely what this lone Amishman on the bald prairies was trying to do. He was still going strong when a pretty young woman (his wife) happened to walk into the room dressed like anyone but an Amishman's wife. Upon seeing us, she darted back into the bedroom at lightning speed. Naturally, I was curious; and by "curious," I mean suspicious and trying to expose his hypocrisy. I asked if they were leaving the faith of their fathers behind them.

"Oh no, no," he said, "she still has all her Amish clothes." A few minutes later, low and behold, out of the room comes this transformed, seemingly submissive, little Amish lady, looking as pert, principled, and proper as ever. It's amazing what a slight alteration of clothes can make.

It's really surprising the things you can learn from someone if you just sit and listen to their many words. In the course of our conversation of maybe a half an hour, and after asking a few seemingly harmless questions, I heard about eight direct westerns from the con (I grew up with a bunch of cousins, and when we didn't trust what someone was saying, we would ask if they were telling us a western, like those of Louis L'Amour or Zane Grey).

One story he told me was especially good. When I inquired about his place of birth, the place he described happened to be the ranch that my family used to farm. It was fascinating to hear him try to describe my old stomping grounds, which he must have visited one time or another. I casually asked him how many years he spent at this location and quickly realized that he was telling us another "western." When we asked about his years in Vietnam and Agent Orange's treatment, he nearly swallowed his coffee cup. That confirmed to me that he had never seen the jungles, humidity, or horrors of Vietnam. His poor face betrayed his lying heart as his expression changed drastically. He was choking, coughing, spitting, and turning beet red as he asked us how in the blazes, we figured he was ever in Vietnam.

I confess we made the mistake of telling him that the local folk filled us in about the support they had given to help and comfort him in his sickness. Later I found out that he returned to the church, threw a terrible fit of anger, and cussed at the little old ladies who were sharing his testimony, who believed in him, who had praised him and extolled him as a true saint.

As we were leaving the yard that day, my two brothers-in-law were on a euphoric high with the demonstration they had just witnessed. I attempted to tell them that this was the professional con doing a little sting operation on the local old folks' home, but they were having none of it. They tried to tune me up and told me that I was just a know-it-all who needed not to be judgmental.

Generally, lessons cost you either time or money, and in this sad instance, a study in discernment cost a lot of people many thousands of dollars. It seemed like everyone I came in contact with had another tale to tell, and story after story started coming in. My buddies from the police force informed me he'd done time in the pen and was a dangerous criminal. His trail covered a vast part of the Eastern seaboard, the Midwest, and all the way out to the West. Everyone we conversed with told us about somebody else that had been swindled. Literally, hundreds of people had been taken to the cleaners by this dude. His plain Amish costume earned this fellow an incredible amount of cash from many of the poor brethren in many different cultures.

For example, he made a fairly decent living for a while, masquerading as a cattle hoof trimmer for several Hutterite dairy farms. According to the fleeced brethren, the con would drive into their yard with a few fifty-dollar bills wrapped around a large bundle of paper to make the money wad look big. While he was trimming the cattle's hooves, he would leave the money roll on the dash of his truck, where all the youngsters could see it, drool over it a little bit, and be tempted to take "just a bill or two." Then, when he got home that evening, he'd take all the paper stuffing out of the money roll and just have the fifties banded together. Bright and early the next morning, down to the Elders' quarters, he would go, with the now shrunken money bundle in hand, claiming the young people stole his funds. He would lay it on real thick.

"I thought you people were Christians! I thought I could trust you! If you can't trust Christians, who can you trust?"

The poor Elders! Now thoroughly intimidated and humiliated, they absolutely couldn't stand the thought of their congregation being branded as common thieves, so they forked over the money and thanked the Good Lord that they were able to be rid of this fellow. This ruse worked very well until the con man met a few Elders who had been through a few rodeos before this man's time and were on to his game. These good folks lived by having all things in common and conceded that they might have the odd petty thief on the colony who would steal now and then as the need arose, but anyone stealing thousands of dollars as the con man claimed was totally ridiculous. After a few colonies realized they had been scammed, they drove the thief from their midst and quickly warned all the other communities.

Meanwhile, back to our construction site, in the small Alberta town, with the fleeced church group. During the middle of the week, my sweet wife would usually go to the local laundromat and wash the crew's clothes. She was doing her thing and just finishing up the job when a brand-new, white Chevy pickup parked in front of the laundromat. Out stepped this fellow with a big Stetson cowboy hat, bright new western shirt, big chrome belt buckle, and fancy cowboy boots. She said she got a strange feeling and said to herself, "I know this guy, I know this guy, I know this guy from somewhere." Then it hit her who it was. Gone were the suspenders. Gone was the old straw hat. Gone were the broad fall pants that were buttoned on the side. Gone were the old Amish shoes, and in their place was a new set of cowboy boots. Yes, everything had been replaced. Out of the beautiful late-model Chevy, in the place of a humble Amish man, stood a handsome cowboy, looking like Roy Rogers himself. Yup, yes, yessiree…

The very finest tale we ever heard of this creative swindler came years later from a revival meeting with a visiting preacher. This gentleman hailed from the far east somewhere in southern Ontario and had come out west to have a week of meetings. One evening, we invited the traveling evangelist to our house for supper and got into the telling of stories. As I begin to narrate the story of the lone Amish chap living on our wind-swept prairies, the far eastern evangelist turned a ghastly white and began to look mighty sickly. After gathering his bearings, he told us that he and this con man once went into business together, many years ago. This con man had been a friend of his, who had grand ideas to begin a welding shop but needed a business partner to help finance the various tools and equipment required to run the shop. Everything was going fine until the evangelist had to go out of town for some meetings. He was only gone for about a week, but all the tools, equipment, and everything was gone when he arrived back home, including his "business partner." Thousands of dollars of specialized machinery and equipment were lost. He said that was the last he saw or heard of the man until I told this story.

It seemed like every place I went, I heard a new story about someone getting shafted by the same man. But before we say to ourselves, "What a hypocrite, what a chameleon, what a crook!" shouldn't we all take a good look at ourselves? How many times have we acted as something we were not? How many times have we said, "Praise the Lord," when we met up with another Christian just because it's the expected thing to say? How about when someone asks us how we're doing? We may be lower than a snake in a wagon rut, yet we put on this sanctimonious air and start using a bunch of cheap Christian clichés to give the impression of having no problems when we're actually burying them. So, before we criticize this man for acting like something he wasn't, let's first examine ourselves and make sure we're not doing the same. At this point, you may be saying, "Wow, that is quite a tale thou dost spin!" But, I say unto thee, "It getteth a whole lot better if thou wilt continue with us for a little while longer."

Let's fast forward a bit from the time of the Amish Con Man to the year 2019. Against millions of people's predictions, a man named Donald Trump was voted in as the 45th president of the United States of America, and the whole world seemed to be turning inside out, and upside down.

Con Man

At sixty some years old, I have been blessed to work alongside a group of really awesome people. The manager of one of the businesses we are involved in has two exceptional daughters, an awesome son, and a top-notch nephew, and we all work together. My delight in life is to build into people's lives, who really want to make a difference and be successful instead of just putting in time.

I had just finished writing the above story about the Amish Con Man and was reading it to our team, including the manager. He listened to the whole thing with a puzzled expression on his face.

"Can I ask you a question?" He asked.

"Sure," I answered.

"What was this Amish fellow's name?"

Before I continue, I should probably tell you that this manager and I are both Canadians. I was born in windy southern Alberta, and my friend was born in southern Ontario. We grew up 2,300 miles apart and he's fourteen years younger than I.

When I told him the Amishman's name he looked at me with a stunned expression, instantly holding up both hands with palms outstretched in disbelief, like he's trying to push the thought away.

All he could get out of his stammering lips was, "No way!"

Con Man - Ray's Fire

After a minute of silence, he exclaimed, "This fellow lived right across the road from where I was born and he's a good friend of my parents, who are both still alive! This is crazy! What are the odds of something like this happening by chance? I've got to go see my parents tonight and tell them this story."

He went to visit his parents and shared the story with them, and they were just as shocked as he was. What's more, they had something to add! "You actually owe this con man your life," they told him. "When you were four months old, we had a house fire, and that man rushed into the house, pulled you out of the crib, and brought you outside."

My friend came to work the next day and filled us all in. "Friends," he said, "if this fellow hadn't been our neighbor, we would not be working together today. My daughters, my son, nor myself. None of us would be here if it weren't for that man."

A hush filled the room as everyone stared at each other, trying to process this new information. I felt the goosebumps rising on my back! Everyone marveled, saying how there absolutely had to be a reason for all this. It couldn't be just chance!

Tell me! What are the odds of meeting this fellow in Alberta when I was a young man trying to make a living…and then hearing this incredible story *from my own fellow worker?!* Years later! Millions of people on this earth but it had to be *him that saved my business partner's life!*

It's almost too incredible to believe!

Our meeting adjourned and everyone went to work, but I just couldn't get the story off my mind. I finally decided I had look at it from a new perspective and I said to myself, "Self, think about this. Jacob from the Bible was a deceiver and a crook, but God never gave up on him. Apostle Paul was a murderer before he met Jesus, but then He used Paul's life to help billions of people. I could give many more examples of people who have found redemption and forgiveness from God, who ultimately became some of the most amazing people on the planet.

I wanted to reach out to this man and say to him, "No matter what you have done, no matter how far you have wandered, there is redemption. I want to personally thank you for running into that burning house and saving that four-month-old baby who today is a dear friend of mine, complete with his precious family. There is so much good in you, and I don't know what happened to you to turn you into a con man. I don't need to know because I do know what you can be if you want to be. Based on the information in these stories, you know who you are, and it won't surprise me a bit if you ended up reading this and found complete redemption."

That's just how wonderful our good, good, Father in Heaven really is!

SON OF A SEACOOK

THE DANGERS OF LEAVING YOUR HUBBY HOME ALONE

I vividly remember that beautiful, warm summer day in the late nineties. Not a breeze stirred, not a cloud graced the endless blue sky, and I was home alone with airplanes on my mind. I stood gazing into that fathomless expanse of azure blue and dreamed of having my very own airplane to fly in any direction that suited my fancy. I looked to the east across the seemingly endless prairie, then to the west to that tall, granite horizon of the majestic Rockies towering into the sky. I dreamed of cruising over them to visit some of my buddies living in the lush, green valleys, deep in their very hearts.

Since that memorable day, I've done a lot of flying in the mountains. You can take an airplane and cover the same distance in an hour that would otherwise take you a day by car. These days, just before I leave on a flight (let's just say to the east coast), I check the tires' air pressure as part of the safety procedure. I say to myself, *"These little tires are going to leave this tarmac, fly over the Great Smokey Mountains, the farms, the freeways, and the cities, and touch down on the Outer Banks of North Carolina, simply because my dream is alive!"* I love doing this before each flight.

I remember often leaving Shelby, Montana, wheels up at 5:00 A.M., then cruising over Yellowstone National Park, past Pikes Peak, right over Truth and Consequences, New Mexico, and finally landing in El Paso, Texas. I'd land again in Ciudad Juarez, Mexico, then lift off again and finally settle down on a gravel road between corn stocks somewhere in the center of old Mexico.

The night before the New York trade towers were destroyed, we were planning a trip into old Mexico, and I told my daughter, who was in flight school with me, that something was wrong. I didn't feel comfortable flying south the next day.

"Dad," she said to me, "are you going to listen to your gut feeling, or are you going to let the mission board pressure you into going?"

I looked at her and said, "Trust me, I'm not flying anywhere tomorrow."

I called the mission board and told them about my apprehension. "I'm not flying tomorrow," I said.

"Maybe you've eaten too many pickles and ice cream," they joked, but I decided to stick with my gut feeling. If I hadn't, we would have been grounded the next day somewhere near Neville, Utah, with a couple of F-16 jets escorting us to the ground. We learned that we would have likely been grounded for days!

I wish I could be granted that kind of positive direction in countless other matters that we are faced with throughout our lives. It seems we could avoid a lot of heartaches, but maybe the heartaches are supposed to happen. After all, God's way is perfect.

One of my friends is a commercial pilot with 3,800 flying hours under his belt. He flies Lear jets and about anything else that gets airborne. He told me that flying could lose its glamour when you're a hired pilot because your employer gets to call the shots. He insists that the best and the most fun is being able to point the nose of the plane in any direction you choose, and when you choose, to fly it.

My beautiful wife and I had the amazing pleasure of raising four children under one roof in a "house that Jack built" long before she said, "*I do.*" It stood in the middle of a 640 acre field in southern Alberta, Canada.

For the next twenty years, there was school tuition, mortgage payments, vehicle payments, doctor bills, socializing bills, and every other bill that comes with raising a family. I seldom had a twenty-dollar bill in my wallet that wasn't spoken for or didn't have a delegated destination that didn't include me! I loved every minute of raising our incredible children, and I could write a book about all our adventures together. Still, after our nest was empty, I finally noticed nice greenbacks with numbers like twenty and 100 that hung around a bit longer since they had no delegated destination. That is, unless my sweet wife became aware of them.

The children were all gone and living on their own, experiencing firsthand how painfully easy it was to provide for themselves and acquire all the things they desired (sarcasm intended). The big house was SO-O-O empty that it echoed several times when you spoke, or when my wife clanged around the kitchen with her stainless-steel pans. The silence became deafening as she and I, smartphones in hand, rocked back and forth on our Lazy Boy™ rockers that boasted a lifetime warranty, no matter how they got abused or trashed. The only sound was the funny creaking they made with each change in position.

Oh yes! Now our children's friends weren't bringing their dogs to our house behind my back and allowing them to jump up on the master bed to pee a little. Pet pigs, cats, dogs, and goats no longer visited our living room to poo-poo behind the couches. The horses were all gone, together with the saddles, the hay bales, the school books, and all the personal belongings of each awesome kid. It was all just memories now. No one was arguing or fighting over toys or chores as their mother and I tried to be impartial referees. Now, all we had to prove we had been there and done that was the photo albums sitting on the coffee table and all the precious memories in our minds.

It sure is crazy how time flies. The older people warned us about it but never explained how fast it actually flew. If you have an opportunity to do something, you better do it, or you'll look up, and it will be gone, gone, *GONE*...and crying won't bring it back.

Like I said at the beginning, even though we were in the middle of raising a family, vainly trying to stay ahead of our bills, airplanes were still on my mind. And I was home alone. I was absentmindedly staring at the beige phone sitting on the counter when someone I had known as a single fellow popped into my mind. I knew this fellow used to be a pilot, but I hadn't connected with him for at least ten years. I called the Telus directory, found his number in Oregon, and placed a call. My old friend, Sam, answered the phone on the second ring.

"Hello," I said, "is this Sam?"

"Sure is!" said the voice on the other end.

"It's Sam Gary from Alberta, Canada."

"I thought I recognized the voice," he answered. (*Wow, wow; after ten years!*)

We visited awhile just to catch up and find out how we were both doing life—how many children we had acquired, if we were happy, if we were still in love with our wives, what businesses we were involved in, and so on, and so forth. Then we got right to the meat, or should I say the main course of the meal? *Ha!*

"Are you still flying airplanes?" I asked.

"Yes, I sure am, and it's a funny thing you asked, because I have a 210 Cessna for sale."

"Have you advertised it yet?" I wondered.

"No, I just decided to let it go, and now you called."

"I might know someone who can use that plane," I told him. My mind was racing through prospects, wishing it could be me, but fully realizing the impossibility of such a dream at my current status.

"What are you asking for it, and what would you give me if I sell it for you?"

He told me the price he needed, then said, "I'll give you fifty hours with an instructor with the fuel and plane included.

"Whew! That's a pretty good incentive!" I said.

We visited some more, then hung up. I started to search my mind which local business might need a plane and a pilot to fly it. I jumped in my truck, drove the thirty miles to town, and stopped at a business place opened by a good friend. Over coffee and conversation, he asked me what I had been up to.

"You don't know of anyone one who needs a nice airplane, do you?" I asked.

"What kind is it? How fast can it go?" he asked. "Funny thing," he said, "my brother and I were just talking about buying one. Have you seen it?"

"No, I haven't," I said.

"Why don't you go check it out, and get back to me?"

"I sure will!" I told him. And that's how I found myself on Amtrack, headed from Alberta to western Oregon.

We met up with our old friend, completely caught up on ten years of time, then we took the plane up for a test run. I had already acquired my private pilot's license at this point in life, so I knew a bit about planes. I soon saw that it was in excellent shape.

So, we called the businessman back home and told him how it all went, and that the motor was still under warranty and the plane was in excellent condition.

"We'll take it," said my friend.

There was a bit of awkward silence, and I inquired, "Really? Just like that?"

"Yes, I'll take it," he repeated. "Tell your friend to send me the paperwork, and I'll pay him immediately."

Just like that, the deal was closed! I was more surprised than anyone. *"Yes! Just do it!"* I thought. *"See what happens!"*

It reminds me of the story of two people who felt the calling to go on a mission to Africa. The one fellow who lived by the ocean kept saying, "God, I'm ready to go to Africa to be a missionary for You," but he got old and died in his cabin without making it to Africa. The other gentleman also lived by the ocean, and like the first chap, he also thought God wanted him to go to Africa, so he set his affairs in order, jumped into the ocean, and started swimming. A passing boat spotted him and gave him a ride across the ocean, and he spent the rest of his years in Africa as a successful missionary.

The Dangers of Leaving Your Hubby Home Alone

Stop talking about accomplishing things. Just go do them!

Now, let's look at this whole scenario from my good wife's perspective. She went to town on a tight budget with the four children, and when she came home, her excited husband was talking a mile a minute. As she was unpacking the groceries, she heard strange words—*210 Cessna, Amtrak, I promise, Oregon,* and a bunch of other frenzied garble that must have sounded to her like some Pentecostal on steroids speaking in tongues.

I thought it was a hard job to sell an airplane to a successful businessman, but can you imagine what it's like to "sell" a broke family man's wife anything to do with an airplane? I quickly realized that here was where I needed to hone every skill and art that I could muster to get her blessing on my wild adventure. My dear wife is an incredible partner that has been stretched for miles during our marriage, but this sudden change of things was almost too much for me, let alone for her!

"Look at me!" she requested.

She stopped what she was doing and stared at me for a long moment. At least she knew she had my full attention. "Start from the beginning," she said. "You're *what?*" she asked. "You bought a ticket to *where? You're* going to be gone *how long? What about me and the children?!!"* (That last one now…ouch…!)

You try answering all that legitimately and rationally. Go ahead, wise guy, show me how it's done! Life don't come easy. Sometimes it's downright hard, and everyone tells you to play it safe. How many men do you know who look back in their lives and say, "Oh my! I'm so glad I played it safe! Life was SO-O-O beautifully monotonous and so boring. But I was safe!"

It turns out my awesome angel-doll of a wife ended up giving me her full blessing! With many hugs and kisses, she sent me away for a month of flying with a military flight instructor stationed on the Oregon coast.

We would land in New Port Bay, eat some clam chowder, do some ground school, and plan another leg of the journey. Then we'd fly over the beautiful Cascade mountains to Bend, Oregon, and do an instrument landing. From Bend, Oregon, down to Redding, California to have supper at the airport, then fly north to the biggest wooden buildings in the world and see where they used to house the blimps of WW2. We flew in the heavy fog, in the pouring rain, through thick clouds experiencing complete whiteouts for long periods of time. Often, we'd be out over the ocean setting up another approach and another landing. We did it all!

The Dangers of Leaving Your Hubby Home Alone
Sam on left - Flight Instructor in the middle

I remember one day, just after landing in Portland, my instructor inquired, "Do you want to go look at the crater in Mount Saint Helens?" A half an hour later, we were looking down into the massive crater that sent millions of tons of ash and rock miles into the sky on that fateful day.

My fine feathered friend, I'm not telling you to be an irrational fool who doesn't face your own reality. I'm just saying that living a safe life because of fear is not the trail I've ever taken or want to take. Life has been an amazing adventure, but God has never let me starve or made me beg, and somehow there's always been a way through the wilderness. *Thank you, Jesus! (and Wifey!)*

All credit goes to the God Who has let me live this extraordinary life. And next to God, I credit my awesome, amazing, smokin' hot wife, who has been there like a rock through thick or thin and has been so strong so many times. A good woman is worth more than priceless rubies, gems, or anything else they can dig out of the rocks. *Ha!*

That fifty hours of instrument flying time that we spent under the hood, staring at a six-pack of gages, has saved my life a few times. I've never regretted the day I made that phone call to buy a plane I couldn't possibly afford. I ended up getting almost ten thousand dollars' worth of valuable instruction, plus an airplane, plus all the fuel from a wild, impossible idea! Maybe I should say it all stemmed from an irresistible urge to fly—soaring with the freedom of an eagle over the mountains, the clouds, the traffic jams full of road rage clientele, and over all the speed traps, speed limit signs, and the high-power lines! Just to *fly free!*

So next time you think you have nothing and nowhere to go, check your heart. If it's beating, you know you're alive! If there's a dream in it, go for it! Then check your hand. If there's a smartphone in it, the sky is the limit of what you can accomplish.

CHINOOK WIND

What is a Chinook wind???
chi·nook /SHə'no͝ok,CHə-/ noun
1. a warm, dry wind which blows down the east side of the Rocky Mountains at the end of winter.

How fast does a chinook wind blow??
In southwestern Alberta, Chinook winds can gust in excess of hurricane force 120 km/h (75 mph). On November 19, 1962, an especially powerful Chinook in Lethbridge gusted to 171 km/h (106 mph). In Pincher Creek, the temperature rose by 41 °C (74 °F), from −19 to 22 °C (−2 to 72 °F), in one hour in 1962.[1]

This story took place on our home farm, where a sidewalk ran through the middle of and separated a cluster of eight homes. "Grandma's House" was on the northwest end, and the church stood a short ways to the east.

Chinook Wind - Community Sidewalk

There was a big old kitchen where we could all eat together and have meetings and gatherings of any kind. Part of the kitchen was a laundry which converted to a butcher house for geese, chickens, or whatever needed to be processed. The ladies also used it to can all kinds of fruit and bag all kinds of vegetables. Us kids would sleep in our own houses at night,

---

[1] (Wikipedia n.d.)

but the moment we got up and hit the sidewalks, we'd be together for the day, roaming around the 3,200-acre farm.

I'm sure that the older generation never had a clue where we were or what we all did all during the long, endless summer days! When we were young, it seemed like summer rolled on forever, and that SO-O-O much happened, but now we realize that the three months of warm weather go by so fast it makes you wonder where it went!

Cousin Billy, one of mother's brother's sons, was a bit younger and shorter than I, but he got into almost as much trouble as I did. Billy loved horses and all animals and had been christened with the nickname *"Mutz"* by his two older brothers. Most people on our farm and the surrounding farms had a nickname due to our use of the CB and the short-wave radios. My handle was *"Shotgun."* Another cousin was nicknamed *"Sidewalk Farmer"* because he didn't really enjoy putting in long hours.

Sidewalk Farmer had a kid brother nicknamed *"Honker"* because, like the geese, he always seemed to be dominating the short-wave radios with his constant chatter. I used to tease him about how I'd re-named him after his parents had christened him at birth, and now even his parents, his aunts and uncles, cousins, and everyone who knew him called him *"Honker."* When I traveled from Alberta, Canada, to Pennsylvania, people wondered if I knew Honker. I'd ask them if they meant Gordie, and they'd say, "No, his name is Honker." So the nicknames sometimes became the real names. That's too funny, but that's how she rolls.

One cousin went by *"Easy Money"* because he always had the best of everything; another one was *"Grease Monkey"* because he always fixed equipment in the shop. There was a *"Honey Cousin"* because if he needed you, he'd butter you up to try and get what he wanted. *"Pajama Joe"* showed up on our farm one day dressed in black and white striped jeans and looking like he came straight out of San Quinten. He wanted work, but he acquired a nickname too.

The large neighboring farm that Pajama Joe hailed from was blessed with four other "Joes" living in the same place. In order to keep track of the Joe you were referring to, it would go something like this—Pajama Joe, Joe the first, Joe the second, Joe the third, and last but not least, Handsome Joe. Ha! Too many "Joes" on one farm, I'd say. Maybe the parents should have communicated a little before naming their kids.

Billy's dad was a preacher, a bishop, an elder, and a father to three sons and a daughter, so Billy and his siblings were always referred to as the *"PKs"* or *"Preacher's Kids."* That meant they were in the limelight and under close scrutiny whether they wanted to be or not!

Billy was probably my closest playmate in all my growing-up years. There wasn't a nook or a cranny of that large farm with which we weren't inextricably acquainted. About thirty interesting old buildings were explored like granaries, chicken houses, quonsets, and wonderful old shanties and barns. We always had an assortment of horses, cows, chickens, pigs, dogs, cats, rabbits, pet owls, uncles, aunts, old maids, cousins, and a crow that could speak because we split his tongue.

If I suggested doing something, crazy or not, Cousin Billy was always ready and eager to try it. One day we were driving illegally on Highway 52 that ran through our farm, and the next thing I knew, those red lights were flashing in my rear-view mirror. I sped up a bit and turned into our farm, and Billy and I leaped out of that old truck and ran into the dark, damp, and old kitchen basement and hid between two freezers. I didn't even hear him coming, but the next thing I knew, the policeman was lifting me up by my ear, and I was squealing like a stuck piglet. To this day, I've been wondering who snitched on our hiding place because that officer should never have found us!

Sometimes we would climb to the hayloft with these lariats that we borrowed from the farm's tack room, and we'd try to get them around the horns of bulls that were in the corral below us. Someone had tied the far end of the lariat around an upright that supported the roof of the building, and a big old three thousand pound bull could have easily jerked the roof support down on top of us if we'd ever have succeeded in snagging his horns.

The week of a big blizzard was when I hitched up my horse to a toboggan and convinced Billy to hop on it. It was blistering cold, maybe minus 40°, but I pulled him into a big, frozen field about three miles from home until we were almost frozen to death. For some reason, we had matches in our pockets and still had the brainpower to start a fire with a bunch of old, dead wood from a grove of trees out in the middle of the bald prairie. The fire kept us from getting permanent frostbite and allowed us to warm up enough to make it home. Forty below? Where were the older people, or should I say our parents?! I will never forget the nightmare of starting that fire with stiff, frozen, numb fingers! But we did get the fire going and did get ourselves warmed up. I think that's why I was so deeply concerned about my own kids growing up; now, my grandkids the same way. I know from experience the things that unsupervised young ones will try. The sky is the limit.

There was a time we drove a yearling bull into a chute, then saddled him up and tried to ride him as though he was a bucking bull. We made homemade explosions out of acetylene and oxygen, stampeding the local feedlot cattle and almost getting ourselves blown up. We had no idea that acetylene gas was unstable out of the bottle because it has its own molecules bumping against each other.

Our Grandmother lived on the same home place with two of her unmarried daughters. Behind their house was a larger row of trees and caragana bushes, and right behind them ran Highway 52. This highway brought a truckload of adventures for us kids right to our doorstep. It was like a pipeline of things coming our way without knowing what would happen next. Thinking back, it seemed like all the good, the bad, or the ugly that entered our world came in via Highway 52!

It reminds me of how the stock market works; if you miss a good ride today, don't sweat it because there's always another one tomorrow. You just have to have a good scanner. A lot of folks live in their past and constantly regret lost "chances of a lifetime." They usually fail to see the opportunities of today that they're missing out on. Today, all we have to do is the very best we can. Grab the bull by the horns, and stand up like a man!

I knew some really bad kids back in the day, and If I had been their parents, I would have soundly whipped them because of some of the tricks they played on the cars flying by on the highway. They would steal eggs from the egg room in poor ol' Grandma's house and try to hit the passing cars. I remember getting on the bus one particular morning after an egg episode. The bus driver was not one bit happy!

"If I knew which one of you little bastards were throwing eggs, I'd whip your asses black and blue!" he stormed. Of course, I happened to know exactly who he was looking for, but I sure wasn't about to tell him! I was so scared I couldn't look him in the face. I was sure glad when that day was over!

How did these "bad kids" get the eggs? It was easy. Someone would go in the front door of Grandma's house and ask for a drink of water or some ice cream or just to visit a bit. The others would sneak into the back of the egg parlor and retrieve a flat or two of eggs. Shame is a shame because this activity brought no future blessings with it.

Another stupid thing these undisciplined brats would do is go down the road about one-quarter mile from our place and put hay bales across the road in the middle of the night. I remember one of these older boys asked me to go with them on a little bike ride, and I was really scared when I saw him set up the bales! He had just finished putting the last bale on the highway when I yelled to him that a car was coming. The grass beside the highway was about a foot and a half deep, so we just lay flat in the tall grass with our bikes and tried not to breathe. Someone came to a grinding halt, got out of the car, and started throwing the bales off the side of the road with great force. Guess where they landed? You've got it! Right on top of us, but still, no one moved. When I looked up, he was gazing out across the field three feet from where the tall grass hid us. I could hear my heart pounding in my ears as I realized what kind of trouble this could have caused had he just looked down by his feet! It reminds me how we often look out into the future, failing to see the things that are right in front of us. I've often wondered who that driver was and what he would have done if he had caught us.

I'm not out to betray names; I'm just giving you an idea of the setting surrounding this story. I'm reminded of another thing that an older cousin enjoyed doing, and he had plenty of chances because lots of folks stopped in and asked for directions. He would visit with the people and then send them way back into the hills in the opposite direction of where they wanted to go. This would give him such an adrenaline rush that he would laugh for a week afterward. If the saying is true that you have to reap what you sow, or what goes around comes around, I wonder how many thousands of miles he's had to drive in the wrong direction since then.

I personally believe that everything goes full circle and that you reap what you sow. If you steal something, you will lose seven times the value of the stolen item. If you lie to people or hurt them in any way, it will come back in some form or another to haunt you. Why not sow the best seeds that we can, and reap a harvest of good? So often, when bad things happened to me, and I was tempted to get angry, I remembered my past and whispered, "Lord, please forgive me." Let him that is without sin throw the first stone.

I need to get to the heart of my story. In the springtime, in southern Alberta, the Chinook wind will start to blow, around 10:00 A.M. Sometimes it will howl all day long for a week or two, sometimes even longer! When you walk towards the west in the middle of the afternoon, your body almost reaches a 45° angle in an effort to stay upright. When the wind suddenly stops, you almost have to relearn how to walk. Haha!

With the old-style telephones we used to have, you couldn't tell who was calling. It was great fun for some of the kids to place a prank call and get a big bang out of messing with people. A friend of mine just flipped through the telephone book and called random numbers. He said he was Professor Malinberg from the Lethbridge University and that he was doing a survey on how the wind in southern Alberta affects the divorce and suicide rate. To his utter amazement, people would start sharing how depressed they were and how hard the wind was on their lives when it blew every day for a month straight. I guess, at his tender age, he never realized the seriousness of the situation and how badly people were hurting.

Somewhere, I was taught to make the best of a bad situation. I know I spent years wondering how I could benefit from the

Chinook. So I built a little cart with a sail and drove it up and down the back roads. This three-wheel cart worked like a charm but happened to be totally illegal, so you were always watching for a police car. Of course, that only added to the fun and excitement of wind sailing. The rest of the local folks would drive past us, give us a thumbs-up, and really thought it was a great idea.

I decided to make a homemade parachute and tie a long rope on it to see if it could lift someone in the air. I ran the idea of getting a man airborne past Billy, and his eyes immediately lit up. "Let's do it!" he said. "Who's gonna be the first one to try it?"

"You're a little smaller than me and about fifty pounds lighter," I reminded him, "So you would be the perfect candidate. Imagine being the first one on our farm to fly up into the atmosphere! I will control the whole flight from the ground, so you don't need to worry."

He didn't say much but nodded uncertainly, which I took as a sign of agreement. We got right to work. We found this old, large, discarded tarp, which was perfect for our experiment of sending a man aloft. The tarp already had holes all along the outside and seemed to be tailored for the job. We found a roll of baler twine and start rigging up the perfect parachute. We were ready for our first human pilot after bringing about thirty strings together and tying them evenly in a secure knot. I tried to make Cousin as comfortable as possible, so I tied the strings to everything on him from the neck down. For some reason, he reminded me of a poor sheep being led to the slaughter, and worse than that, it was coming from a friend! Talk about the ultimate act of usury!

I had no sooner got him all ready for the launch when the wind became even stronger. I had the end of the 100 foot rope securely fastened to a fence post with the other end tied in a knot just above Billy's head. I told him to stand facing the wind for a perfect take-off and to get ready for a nice ride. I reassured him of the strength of thirty pieces of baler twine. Now that I'm sixty with a real pilot's license under my belt, I understand just how lethal the situation was for my poor cousin. It makes me very happy today that it didn't cripple him, or worse yet, end his sojourning on this earth.

I told Cuz that I would open the tarp to the wind as soon as he nodded that he was ready to fly. The very split second that Billy nodded his head and I pulled open the top of that tarp, the wind grabbed it ferociously and jerked my poor cousin thirty feet into the air as effortlessly as a bird in flight. I was about to scream a victory shout when the wind suddenly shifted direction, sending Billy flying sideways with great speed. The strings of baler twine started popping and snapping; the tarp began shredding like a piece of onion skin as it smashed poor Billy on the ground about sixty feet from lift-off. Another fierce gust jerked him and the shredded tarp back off the ground the second time and let him fall again, hopelessly tangled in baler twine in the fifty-mile per hour, southern Alberta, Chinook wind!

Chinook Wind - Homemade Wind Cart

You cannot imagine my immense relief when Billy slowly, stiffly got up on his feet and walked toward me, asking me to release him from the fetters that bound him. He said he was hurting something awful but didn't think anything was broken or sprained. I said, "Billy, you sure are the right stuff! You'll make a fine pilot someday, but now you just relax while I clean up this mess!"

I'm not sure what you're thinking by now, but I think every red-blooded young boy has dreamed of flying at one time or another in his life. It's in our DNA; it's in our blood! That's why we gaze intently into the blue sky above and long to ride the wind, just like the birds!

So, with the current launching experiment behind us, I wanted to present Billy with my new idea of finding a stronger tarp, some new nylon rope, and maybe jumping off the barn roof. Somehow I knew that day was bad timing for my presentation. I was pretty sure that poor Mutz had enough excitement for one day.

Maybe you think I'm a mean, nasty bully taking advantage of someone younger than myself. But that's not true! I'm a true engineer, and if something happened to me, all my brilliant ideas would cease. Test pilots are a dime a dozen, says Chuck Yeager. They can be replaced, and you can always find more of them, but true engineers? They are a rare breed indeed.

LOS ANGELES – HAROLD & I

Back in the nineties, a friend of mine received an order for 300 grandfather clocks. He was trying to provide work for folks in Romania who made these beautiful hand-carved creations. Long story short, the people he was trying to find jobs for called him pretending to be a large company and ordered *a lot* of clocks. So he set the wheels in motion and started building literally hundreds of them, complete with *Black Forest Clock Works* as the operating mechanism. When he realized it was a fake order, he asked if I could help him sell these beautiful gems to stores across America.

Away we went, doing trade shows from Seattle, Washington to Denver, Colorado to South Carolina, and everywhere in between. Talk about putting on the miles! On one particular trip, we started from Lethbridge, Alberta, and took a load of clocks to northern Indiana. From there, we traveled to Toronto, Ontario. Next, we drove down to Dansville, Virginia along the beautiful Skyline Drive to pick up a load of clockworks, then back to Toronto where we picked up eighteen more clocks. Finally, we headed back to Los Angeles via Alberta.

Somehow I had convinced my friend Harold to come along on one of these trips to help me drive. We would take turns behind the wheel while the other guy slept, and then we'd trade off again. It sure beat solo driving and ate up the miles in a hurry.

My story begins after Harold had driven from Montana to Meadow, Utah, a couple of hours south of Salt Lake City. He pulled off at a truck stop around 4:00 A.M. and said, "Sam, it's your turn to drive. I'm going to catch myself some shut-eye."

Now you guys probably don't know my friend Harold, but you probably know someone like him. The man is usually smiling broadly and has a terrific sense of humor, which makes his company very enjoyable. Harold needed a good laugh at least three times a day, and many times that was just a beginning.

Harold's absolute favorite sport is golfing, so if he has a faraway look in his eyes he's probably dreaming of some green golf course down in Arizona. *Ha!* He told me a story about three guys that went golfing. One poor fellow named Jake was hit in the head by a golf ball and knocked out cold at the beginning of the game. What did they do? They had waited all week to play! For the rest of the day, it was unanimously decided to hit the ball, drag Jake, hit the ball, and drag Jake. That's just a glimpse of Harold's exciting priorities with a bit of history tucked in.

Hit the ball, drag Jake. Hit the ball, drag Jake. Hit....

So now it was my turn behind the wheel. I went into the truck stop, bought a coffee and some dill-flavored *Spitz TM,* stretched, yawned, and did a few jumping jacks to make sure I was fully awake. It was still dark outside when I started the four-door Ford F350 and glanced into the back seat. There was old Harold, fast asleep.

"Man he must be exhausted!" I thought. "Took him five minutes to fall asleep."

I thought it very strange that he was sleeping on the floor with one leg up across the seat. I didn't know if my old friend had been kicked out of bed so often that this was a familiar position or what. But I figured it was none of my business how he slept. He had done a lot of miles and deserved to sleep in any position he wanted to.

What a peaceful Sunday morning it was! As we pulled up some of those steep grades just before St. George, Utah, the old diesel was purring along, and I could hear the faint whistle of the turbo now and then. I considerately made sure the music was just above a whisper and wouldn't disturb Harold. Of course, no phone rang to wake him up either since this was before the days of cell phones.

Finally, after a couple of hours and a good 100 miles down the road, the eastern sky started to show some pink and I could see my surroundings a little better. I couldn't believe how soundly a body could sleep! No snoring, no heavy breathing, no sleep-talking, not a sound!

I glanced back to make sure that Harold hadn't died on me, only to see that his leg had fallen off the seat and he was now entirely on the floor. I slowed down, pulled over on the shoulder, and checked to see if my buddy was still breathing.

The back seat of that four-door, F350, seven-liter, Ford dually was completely empty! I was alone in the truck. Just me and a few million amused angels.

I screamed, I cried, and I shrieked with laughter. My side hurt, my belly hurt, and after a coughing fit, I thought I'd better behave myself before I hurt something. I know the angels in Heaven laughed with me that day. I don't ever expect to top that pleasurable experience of being alone—not in this lifetime!

Now let's hear my buddy Harold's perspective. He had decided to go into the truck stop and phone his wife. He says he handed me the key as I was coming out of the coffee shop towards the truck. When he saw the truck start moving, he asked his wife, "Is Sam trying to play a trick on me?" But when I started up the ramp, he ran after me as fast as he had ever run. He was just about to grab the back of the trailer latch when he realized that that's the worst place he could possibly find himself, hanging on to the door handle and standing on his toes on a three-inch ledge, on the back of a clock trailer, going down the freeway at seventy miles per hour! So he gave up the chase and watched me cruise away, then walked back to the truck stop.

Meanwhile, I pulled over at the next fuel station and phoned the state troopers. Yes, Harold had been calling them time and time again, and they were all out looking for me. They gave me a number to call Harold, and he picked up on the very first ring.

"How far down the road are you?" he asked.

"About 100 miles."

"You're going to have to turn around and come back Sam," he said.

"But that will turn into a four-hour mistake! Can't you hitch a ride with one of the truckers?" I wondered.

"I've already tried but I'll try again; just give me a minute," he agreed.

A minute later the phone rang. "I've got a ride," Harold said happily. "What's your mile marker?"

A couple of hours later, I woke to the sound of Jake-brakes on the freeway, and there came Harold, running towards the truck.

As soon as Harold jumped into our truck he said, "That was an interesting guy! He's a Mormon and instantly started to tell me about Joseph Smith, and the Mormon church, and that I really need to join them"

"Oh ya? What did you tell him?"

"I asked him if he realized it was Sunday, and if the Mormons were allowed to work."

"And…?"

"'Well I'm a jack Mormon,' he said, 'but I give ten percent, so everything should balance out.' Then I asked him if that was his way of buying God off and he said not really. He was just hoping his good deeds outweighed the bad ones."

"Then what did he say?"

"I asked him if he didn't think God was more interested in what he did with the other ninety percent than what he did with ten percent. We pretty much rode in silence after that, but there were no converts today—not for me or for that Mormon trucker who was searing his conscience by driving on Sunday!"

Out of this whole ordeal, we got the laugh of the day plus had a good discussion with a kind trucker who helped us out. And several hours later we were a team again, heading down the freeway towards Las Vegas and Los Angeles.

Just before Las Vegas, it was Harold's turn to drive again. I had noticed that the brakes seemed awfully weak, but I figured if we took it easy we could probably make it home.

"Watch the brakes, my friend," I warned him. "Seems like they're way too weak."

I had no sooner spoken than the traffic came to a complete stop right in front of us. I looked over at Harold just in time to see his posterior rise completely off the seat as he put everything he had on them brakes. No matter how hard the brother pushed, I knew we could never stop in time. Thank God for a wide left shoulder!

My buddy swerved over just in time, bringing sixty thousand dollars' worth of grandfather clocks and an F350 dually with a brand-new trailer to a halt about five car-lengths past the backend of the last vehicle in that Las Vegas traffic jam!

Harold was pretty shaken up. "We need to get new brakes on this rig ASAP!" he declared.

We continued on, keeping a little further behind, and traveling a little slower on Highway I-15. Hours later, we arrived in Los Angeles, right during rush hour.

I was using this old 8-mm movie camera, filming the sites of the big city and praying that there would be no more close shaves 'til we reached our destination. I felt better just knowing that the trailer would be a lot lighter, just as soon as all the clocks were unloaded.

We came around a curve, and there, right smack dab in the middle of I-10 sat an old hippie van at a complete stop. There was a solid line of traffic to our left, and a solid line of traffic to our right, with no place to turn.

I've got to hand it to our dear brother, he did his very best. Not only did his posterior come off the seat a minimum of five inches, but he also reached over with his left leg and smashed the emergency brake solidly against the truck's firewall. No doubt he was thinking that's all she's got, and there ain't no more to give, as we smashed into this multi-colored hippy van and sent it flying into the other lane.

Bang! Bang! BANG!

More and more cars collided. Talk about a sinking feeling. Suddenly our heavy trailer unhooked, the bumper snapped off, the right front fender crumpled like tin foil into the wheel, and all around us, I-10 west was shutting down.

Soon the police arrived, coming towards us from the wrong direction. I got out of the truck as the state trooper approached. "I see you boys are from Canada," he said. "Are there any big bucks up in your neck of the woods? I'm looking for a connection to come up there and do some hunting."

Wow, that sure put us at ease.

These guys were so cool, so professional as if this was no big deal. Just another interesting day in California. I guess it's their job. It's what they do.

As fast as we could, we grabbed our toolbox, bolted on the bumper, hooked up the trailer with the correct ball hitch, manually pried the fender away from the front wheel and we were ready to roll. (My hired man had put on a two-inch ball hitch instead of a two and five-sixteenth one which is why the trailer came unhitched.)

The trooper was talking with the hippies in the van and soon came back to our truck. "Looks like you gentlemen are ready to go," he said. "The van you hit has no license, no insurance, and no identification. Thankfully there were no injuries, so you're good to go."

"You're driving, Sam!" Harold exclaimed.

"No way," I told him. "It's still your turn."

He got in, buckled up, put the truck in gear, and off we went. He was holding a full can of Coke in his right hand and steering with the left. "Can you help me with this tab?" he asked. I reached over, popped the tab, and watched in horror as the can exploded all over the seat, Harold, and I.

The look on the brother's face was priceless. It was similar to that of *Wile E. Coyote* as he runs into a freight train for the tenth time while trying to catch *Beep Beep* the roadrunner.

We hadn't covered a full mile when a car pulled alongside, laying on his horn. I looked back to see billowing clouds of black smoke coming off our wheels. "Can you release the emergency brakes, Bro?" I asked calmly.

A week after returning home to Alberta, we sold that black, F350, 7.3 liter Ford dually pickup truck. And this is my version of the story. Maybe you should get Harold's, too.

And the clocks? We unloaded those eighteen beautiful grandfather clocks, and they were in perfect condition! Not even a scratch. The last leg of the trip was a lot better than the first! Maybe because we gave the angels a good laugh! *Ha!*

RIGHTEOUS JIM

I guess this title sort of sets the stage of the following story. It's called *"Righteous Jim"* because every time we'd get into trouble back on the home farm, the older folks would say, *"Why can't you be like little Jim?"* Or they would say, *"If you belonged to me, I would certainly teach you how to behave!"*

They were SO-O-O busy trying to raise other people's kids that they forgot about their own. Never a good way to operate!

I have discovered, that if you do a good job with the children God has given you, you'll have a full-time job, and still do a lot of sweating and searching for answers. I gladly admit that I'm still searching for answers, and the older I get, the shorter my answers are. Love God with all your heart, soul, and mind, and love your neighbor as yourself. You'll finish okay!

Never judge the wine in its fermenting state. Wait until it is fully finished fermenting.

Righteous Jim was always held up to us as an example of what a young person should be. He always was and still is a good guy and a real gentleman with an amazing sense of humor. I'm not at all disagreeing that young people need good mentors in their lives, but one thing I've learned after sixty years is that people are people are people, *are just people,* and we're all made of the same exact stuff! The moment you elevate someone on a pedestal, you're setting him up for a big fall. This is a fact, and if you don't believe me, just live a little longer, and life will teach you the truth.

We were raised in a very conservative setting. We were not allowed a television and only watched it when we could slip down to the neighbor's house on a Thursday night to sneak in *Old Ironside,* or *The Streets Of San Francisco,* or maybe *Starsky and Hutch,* or even *Andy Griffith.* We all worked for the common good of the farm and basically had all things together.

So when my uncle came up to me and asked if I would like to go to Minnesota with Cousin Jim to pick up a tractor, I was ecstatic! It was a first real shot at being off the farm, having unsupervised freedom away from all the work with no one controlling or scrutinizing our daily activities.

"I'll give you the farm credit card if you'll do the job," Uncle promised. Very sweet words to my young ears and I didn't need any persuasion to consent. The credit card was an American Express, and when I stuck that beautiful green card in my pocket, I remember thinking, *"Are we ever gonna have some fun…ya ya, baby!"*

I figured I was not sent on this trip by myself for a reason. Jim was along to keep me in check. At least that's what I thought at the time.

We get the truck all ready to go, listened to all the warnings from the adults about the big, bad, old world, and finally, we were allowed to hit the road.

Talk about excitement! Pulling away from the farm all on our own; nobody to tell us every move to make; and best of all, an American Express credit card with a huge amount of credit. If I remember correctly, the very first stop was only four hours down the road from the old farm. Sure, it was only a short haul but a big red and black sign on a building caught our attention pretty quick! *Pizza Hut!*

You've got to remember folks, that this was our first time off the big farm with the big, wild, wonderful world sprawled out in front of us, an American Express credit card with no limits in our pocket, and all kinds of adventure beckoning to us! We ate two big pizzas, drank wa-a-a-a-y too much Coca Cola, had an awesome time, and hit the road.

Growing up on the farm and eating a steady diet of homegrown produce of all kinds had us youngsters pretty healthy. So, after two large pizzas, five refills of Coca-Cola, and half an hour of driving, Jim said, "Man, oh man, I'm so tired, I'm afraid I'm gonna fall asleep behind the wheel."

I have seen it so often, that I totally believe that there's tremendous power in the spoken word. He had no sooner declared how terribly sleepy he was, than I looked up and noticed the flashing neon lights of a motel, just off the exit!

"I agree!" I said to Jim. "We better get a motel, get a good night's rest, and hit the road in the morning!"

Now, Righteous Cousin Jim didn't need any convincing. He whipped the truck into the motel parking lot, officially five whole hours from home. We grabbed our suitcases, locked the truck, and purchased a motel room. It was only four-thirty in the afternoon, but we were convinced that we should rather be safe than sorry, and definitely not drive tired!

Funny thing, as soon as we checked in, all fatigue vanished just like that. That old black and white television got smokin' hot entertaining two movie-starved young guys who had never been allowed the opportunity. After four or five movies, I fell asleep around 2:00 A.M., totally exhausted. Three hours later, I jerked awake, wondering groggily where I was, only to see Cousin Jim still glued and transfixed to the boob tube!

If I remember right, Liz Taylor was lighting up the screen, young and so beautiful like she used to be. It looked like Righteous Cousin Jim was in a mesmerized trance, and after forty years I still have this picture of him in my mind. I eventually fell back to sleep and never did find out when he finally hit the sack. The next thing I remember was someone pounding on the motel door threatening to charge us for another night if we didn't get out in five minutes.

I looked over at the clock beside the bed, heard this awful groan from Cousin Jim as he rolled over, then slowly sat up, holding his head. "Got an awful headache," he moaned.

"Hey! It's twelve-thirty and I'm hungry as a bear," I told him. "What do you wanna do for breakfast?"

"You're gonna have to do some driving," he groaned. "I feel wasted for some reason."

We opened the air-conditioned motel room door only to be hit by a heatwave as we climbed back into the old Ford Louisville truck, where it was 20° hotter than outside. Soon we were flying along Highway 2 from Shelby, Montana to northern Minnesota. If my memory serves me correctly, we put in a good three hours before we decided it was high time to get some grub.

"We really need to find a motel with a swimming pool tonight," Jim decided in the course of conversation. "With a heatwave like this, we really need to cool off!"

I had no sooner said that I was hungry when a large, neon sign caught our eye! Guess what it said! You're right…there was good old Pizza Hut right off the exit, and right behind it was a beautiful, new Howard Johnson motel with a super-sized swimming pool!

"There's not a shadow of a doubt that Someone's looking out for us," I pointed out to Jim. "They have to be!"

Cousin Jim looked at me in the most sheepish way and asked, "What will the old folks think of us? We're not even halfway to our destination and this is already day two?"

This all took place long before the days of smartphones, so people were only in contact if they had to be. It was nothing like nowadays. At seventeen, I left the farm and went to live in Missouri for about nine months and very seldom heard from anyone. Folks never knew if I was dead or alive, and probably figured that no news was great news. Think of all the brave pioneers who went west on the wagon trains and were never heard from again.

So, once again that afternoon, we gorged ourselves with pizza, coke, cheese sticks, and marinara sauce without the slightest worry of how we'd be able to push all this through our poor bodies. We were definitely uneducated about the fundamentals of life, even on how bodies worked. All we knew was we weren't gonna miss this opportunity of a lifetime!

What a beautiful motel! It was twice as expensive to be sure, but we figured this didn't happen every day.

"What trunks are we gonna use?" Cousin Jim asked.

That's when we found a vending machine that read, *Durable plastic swimming trunks. One size fits all. $3.00.*

We went back to the motel room and as fast as we could, we jumped into our swimming trunks. Cousin Jim had no problem, but mine were so tight they cut off my circulation at certain points. I pulled and jerked and jumped and finally got them up to my waist.

"Let's go!" I yelled and started running down the long, carpeted hallway toward the swimming pool. The pool was quite crowded and had a diving board at least six feet high. I could not wait! I got up on the diving board, bounced as hard as I could, and did a backflip into the water, splashing all over the place. I came up for air and gave my head a quick shake to flip the water from my face, and I notice that everybody was laughing.

"*Well,*" I thought. "*If they think that was so spectacular, wait till they see my next move!*"

I repeated my performance at least five times, each time trying to improve my incredible style. Instead of swimming, folks were lined up along the side of the pool, giving me this tremendous applause every time I dove. It didn't quite make sense. I mean, hadn't they seen people dive before? Come on now, these total strangers were laughing and carrying on like I was some Olympic diver. And because I had such an appreciative audience, I started to bow before every performance. They literally shrieked.

My Righteous Cousin Jim, who was also standing on the side of the pool, was laughing so hard he couldn't speak. I edged over to him after one amazing high dive and kinda whispered, "Why is everybody acting so crazy and applauding me? I can't believe how easily these English people are entertained!"

"It's just because you're so good," he assured me, with tears in his eyes. "They've never, *ever* seen such talent in a farm boy!"

"Well, why don't you go show them how it's done, too?" I wondered. He just shook his head.

"Naw! You're way better," he said.

Thinking back, I can hardly believe that Cuz actually let me climb up that diving board ladder again. And that he just stood there and laughed like an idiot.

At this point, I had run out of ideas, so I figured I would try a triple backflip. The resounding applause was giving me courage that I hadn't been able to muster before. I was just about ready to dive when Righteous Jim cupped his hands around his lips and expected me to become an instant expert in lip reading. After three or four tries I figured out these words, *"You're pants are split!"*

I realized with a shock that they've all been laughing at my bare-ass performance, especially when I did that Chinese bowing thing!

Get the picture—I'm perched six feet high on the diving board when my lights come on and in desperation I look down, only to realize that my durable plastic swimming trunks have disintegrated into a loincloth that totally failed to hide the exposed beauty from the English world.

That was the end of the Chinese bowing and the double backflips! I was far too embarrassed to crawl back down off the diving board so I quickly ran off the end, never looking to the right or left as folks got one more good look. I literally walked on water getting out of that expensive Howard Johnson swimming pool, located somewhere between Shelby, Montana, and St. Paul, Minnesota!

Cousin Jim staggered into the room like someone who wasn't all there in the head, threw himself back on the bed, and laughed and laughed and *laughed!* Helplessly. It really started to bug me.

I can never remember a time in my entire life when I was so utterly embarrassed, as Righteous Jim, between gasps, described my half-hour stunts for a room full of strangers…almost butt naked.

Somewhere in America, on this very night, the American flag is still flying and representing our freedom. But also somewhere this very night, maybe around campfires or drinking parties, or in circles where old friends get together, there's a story being told about a wild, half-hour performance by a clueless sixteen-year-old kid who put on a show the likes of which Hollywood has never topped!

THE HOUSE THAT JACK BUILT

For you to see and understand the setting and dire situation that I'm endeavoring to put into words, I must do some explaining. When my sweetheart and I first got married in 1980, we moved into this little house, which stood on the top of a hill, right out in the middle of a vast 640-acre field. At the far end of this field was another vast field, and then another, and after that still another. From our living room window, you could see so far that you could watch your dog run away from home for two days.

I made the horrible mistake of building a house before I had a wife, and I later found out that I didn't have a clue about matching colors or a host of other things. For instance, I installed a blue tub in the small bathroom that I paid practically nothing for. I was proud that it was ready to use—it only cost thirty dollars and my time, which I considered to be free. I then found a brown bathroom vanity, complete with a yellowish color sink already mounted in it. A little bit of plumbing, a few screws to tie it to the wall, and we were in business. Not bad for a $20 bill. Now, all I needed was a commode, and a person could sh--, shave, shower, and shampoo all in one room. Someone gave me a lovely white commode, and an hour later, we had it installed. Big goosebumps coursed back and forth, up and down my body as I stood back and examined the house that some fortunate lady would have the privilege to move right into and turn it into a home.

Finally, the day came when the house was nearly complete, except for a whole bunch of little things that we could finish later. Now it was time to party. It was time to get married to this lady, who had the biggest, most beautiful blue eyes I had ever seen. She happened to live some 2,300 miles away, and I was to bring her home to be with me. *Ya, ya, baby,* was I excited!

My gorgeous bride was in for quite the surprise when I finally brought her from the beautiful, lush, green hills of Pennsylvania back to a little house in the middle of a 640-acre stubble field. Our new home had no grass, no running water, no porch, no yard, no yard light, not even steps up to the front door or down the five-foot drop of the back door. It had only a plowed field.

I must admit, I did get a little nervous when she mentioned that she would have liked to pick out the house's colors and furnishing, and that was before she had ever seen inside of it.

But for me, all I could think was, "I have the most stunning, beautiful lady that I've ever seen, and she's my wife? For life? How good can it get? Pinch yourself, dude." I had fallen, I was mesmerized, I had lost it, I was under her spell.

The evening shadows were just starting to fall before we entered our new home-to-be, where we would start our journey of life together. Because we had a little daylight left, we spent a short time walking around our new house and discussing how we could start to landscape and create a nice yard.

The moment finally arrived for her to see her new home as I helped her climb into the three-foot-high doorway that was still in need of outside stairs and a fresh coat of paint. This grand entrance was some forty years ago, and I can still see the expression in her eyes when she first saw the bright yellow linoleum and the brand new, dark maroon, 1-inch shag carpet at the top of our split-level home.

She looked at me for a long moment, as though she was going to speak, but didn't say a thing. She then mounted the stairs, went down the short hallway, and looked into the blue kitchen. I had gotten a whole bunch of cabinets for next to nothing, simply because they were mismatched, and we found places to install each and every one while saving a ton of money. My beautiful bride then proceeded down the hallway and entered the bathroom. From there, she just stared at it for what seemed like five minutes. To break the awkward silence, I said, "All we need to do is drill the well, and the water will be running, sweetheart."

Again, she looked at me with this questioning gaze and smiled, but still didn't speak a word. It was then that I looked into those beautiful blue eyes and perceived that they had some moisture brimming around them. My heart just leaped for joy as I thought about her emotions being so stirred by the love she must have had for me for giving her this brand-new house, which had been built with pure love for the woman of my dreams. Yes, yes, this was my perspective, at this stage of holy matrimony.

Now my sweetheart was the best woman that a man could ever find! She was (and still is) a saint in my eyes. She didn't cuss, say mean words, and smiled through her tears. Even when she was hurt, she was so tenderhearted. The words of the song that Waylon Jennings used to sing took on a brand-new meaning for me, "She's a good-hearted woman."

I've now lived with her for some forty years. I am still trying to get to know what she likes, what she doesn't like, what she expects, what she doesn't expect, when she's hot, when she's cold, how much cream to put in her coffee, what she's really saying when she says she's tired, when she wants her feet rubbed, when she wants to be by herself, when she asks if she looks fat, what to say, and what not to say, and a whole array of other things a man needs to know so he can have a successful marriage. I now understand that the moisture I had seen brimming in those beautiful blue eyes of hers when I first introduced her to our new home and had perceived as tears of love and joy were closer to tears of confusion.

Who in the hell ever picked out the colors, carpets, flooring, trim, lights, countertops, and the cabinets for this house?

My dear friend, if you can learn anything from my mistakes, please do. Then all the hard work of writing this will be pay enough for me just for you to be spared the agony. A woman's house is her nest; it's an expression of her extended self. Every nook, cranny, corner, and every closet is her rightful domain, and she will dominate it. Nothing ever misses her eye. Words that men say, like, "That's good enough," or "Is it date night?" when you've just violated her sense of beauty by bringing some mismatched piece of furniture into her nest, is an act of insanity.

The House That Jack Built

Does this make any sense to you? Think about it. Make love to her, and she'll give you a child. Give her a house, and she'll turn it into a home. Bring her groceries, and she'll make you a meal. Everything you give a good woman, she'll reproduce. That's why she's called the womb-man.

Another thing you do with a new bride is never move her into a house with no running water. Never, never, under any circumstances, do this.

We had to haul our water when we first started. We would open the back door and hope no one showed up while we were doing our thing. For a man, that is easy. He just whips it out, waits a few seconds, then locks it back up, and he's done, but with a lady, things aren't that easy.

I remember that one *"blistery, blustery day,"* as Winnie the Pooh would say when we had just ordered a load sod to be laid around the perimeter of our new home. I was outside in the front of our house, telling the three men who had come to help us lay sod that we would start in the back of the house, then work our way around to the front. I told them we better get moving, so the wind wouldn't dry out the sod. If that happened, the grass would die, and all our work would be in vain.

I should have first gone into the house and told the ladies who were working inside that the crew had all arrived, but I didn't. Hindsight is always 20/20, I guess.

The men headed towards the back of the house, about the same time one of the ladies was doing a balancing act out the back door, using the restroom. I opened the front door just as the wind ran through the house, slamming the back door into the backside of a balancing young lady. She was propelled out the door with her panties around her ankles. She dropped five feet down to the ground, just as the crew came around the back of the house. No, no, no, this should have never happened, never, never, never.

So now, all the working men could see was a young lady with her dress dragging on the ground, calmly doing a duck waddle walk and pulling out a few

The House That Jack Built - Working on the Basement

insignificant weeds around her as she stayed squatted close to the ground. The men couldn't see the pants around her ankles, slowing her speed. They told her she didn't need to pull the tiny weeds because the sod would cover them, but she answered them never a word. So, what did they do? They just moved on and went to work, then turned around, and she was gone, lickety-split, just like that.

I think about it some days when I'm reminiscent over the past, what must go through the men's minds. Do they ever go back to that fateful day when we were laying sod around our new home? To the day when they encountered one of the strangest things they'd ever seen - a beautiful young lady doing a duck waddle, with her dress dragging on the ground. Yes, I wonder what they think. I can see them holding their chins, with their feet crossed, looking off into the distance, and slowly shaking their heads, as they go, "Hm-m-m-m."

I guess she must have looked around, found her moment, jerked up her pants, and came flying through the front door where I happened to be innocently standing, absolutely oblivious to the mortification she had just experienced.

The first thing I said to her was, "Where did you come from? I thought you were in the house." She ran right past me without even replying, then smashed the door behind her as she entered some back bedroom in the recesses of our new home.

I still can't figure women out, especially what is running through their minds to make them act so strangely. But, I could not wait around because we had a trailer load of sod that was drying out and needed to be laid.

BOTTOMLESS WHISKEY

I remember a fine, single, older gentleman named Frank who immigrated from Holland to Canada. Interesting note; Holland is way below sea level. As the old saying goes, *"If you want to stop the Dutch from their daily activities, just blow up the dikes!"*

Remember the little boy in our second-grade reader who was walking home from school and stumbled upon a hole in the dike? It was only a trickle so he stuck his thumb in the hole and sat there all night, almost freezing to death, but his heroic deed supposedly saved Holland from being submerged!

Frank had experienced all the horrors of WW2, which was supposed to be the war that ended all wars. He had witnessed and survived Hitler's demented thousand-year reign dream about creating the perfect Arian race, without spot, wrinkle, or blemish. He had heard the hard speeches as Hitler spun his vicious web around the minds of the millennials of the day and how he had filled their heads with an impossible pipe dream. Yes, he had watched how the innumerable masses of people literally made the ground tremble as they screamed, *"Heil Hitler!"* while thrusting out their right hands in a salute of total worship and mindless submission—even unto death.

Frank had watched this dictator's twisted dreams start, and he had watched as they all crashed and burned! He had an endless reservoir of good stories that he could tell a bunch of us wide-eyed, German farm boys during coffee break. He admitted that many times when he was trying to sleep, he could still hear bombs exploding and tracer bullets whining as the madness of the war lit up the night skies of his fatherland.

All because of one lone, Jew-hating psychopath.

I can picture Frank in my mind, scratching his chest with vigor every time he'd tell us something funny. He would start laughing and scratching till the joke fizzled out. The funnier the story, the more viciously he'd scratch that now leather-toughened, smoke-cured chest of his, toughened by a million or more roll your own, Export A cigarettes. Frank could be driving a tractor in a howling Chinook wind, reach in his pocket with his right hand, simultaneously pull out a wrapper, dig into his tobacco sack with the same hand, and roll a cigarette from start to finish—all with one hand!

I was so impressed. I'm sure Frank never dreamed that he would someday be the main character of a good story! But I truly do miss him, his eccentric ways, and the many good memories we built together. He deserves so much more than just a chapter in someone's book because of his integrity and faithfulness.

Frank, my friend, I missed you when that chapter closed and writing this story has stirred a lot of good emotions from when I was just a kid. You took time out for me and enriched my life in so many ways.

We ran a commercial cattle feedlot on our farm and ranch, and Frank was the man in charge. He managed it well, living in a trailer house right on the premises. Through the winter months, some of us young boys would be delegated to help him. That included caring for sick animals, bedding cattle down daily with fresh, yellow straw bales that we'd have to break apart, and using pitchforks to spread it into a fluffy layer on the elevated pile where the cattle slept. It took thousands of bales to keep those cattle warm! We mixed silage made of rolled oats and rapeseed oil in the feed wagon to keep the cattle from bloating, then filled the troughs so they would never run out of feed. We would start feeding the newly weaned calves with hay and just a small portion of the grain, but keep adding more and more grain until they were on full feed.

This might be hard to believe, but one day when the temperature dropped to minus 58° Fahrenheit, the propane began to jell in the tanks. My ingenious dad built a log fire right underneath the tank to get the propane back into a liquid stage so it would flow into all the buildings on the farm. I asked him if he wasn't afraid that the tank would blow up, but he explained that propane inside the tank was so cold, that even with a fire right under the tank, the steel only got slightly warm. He claimed there was no danger at all.

In the winter, we used various fuel additives in our vehicles because of the intense cold. If you didn't take the necessary precautions, you could end up paying dearly. One day, we were driving along the highway in a bad snowstorm and noticed an old blue Pontiac on the shoulder with the windows fogged shut. We pulled over to check inside and here was a mother stranded with five little children! They would certainly have frozen to death had we not found them and hauled them to town. Her gas line was frozen solid and the engine oil was so thick that the engine wouldn't crank. Of course, there were no cell phones around yet so she couldn't call for help. Often, we would hear on the news how someone was found frozen to death. Now back to my buddy Frank!

Every day at break time, Frank would invite us into his trailer house to warm up with a strong coffee sweetened with fresh honey, and to snack on small pieces of special cheese from Holland. I still dream about that cheese. After coffee and cheese, we'd finish up by rolling our very own Export A cigarettes, and enjoy a good, unfiltered smoke, hear a few more stories about the old country, and ho, ho, ho, ho, back to work we'd go. I knew when the break was over because inevitably Frank would say, "Boys! We're not getting any of our work done while sitting in here!"

Frank always had some hard liquor stashed away in the recesses of the old trailer house! We had a lot of folks from the east come out west, and a certain young fellow who helped us at the feedlot had no respect for anyone's privacy. He knew exactly where the whiskey stash was located. Sometimes, Frank would go to town to stock up on groceries and whatever else was running low. As soon as this disrespectful chap would see him leave, he would raid poor Frank's trailer. He'd borrow a fresh pack of tobacco, eat a few pieces of cheese, then go for the gold—the whiskey!

Maybe the reason this happened is because of a simple fact. In the winter we had to put additives into our machines so they would function properly. If you poured a light-duty oil into a motor so the starter could crank it in cold weather; if you put an additive into the gas tank so the gas wouldn't freeze; if you put a heat bulb into the watershed so the cows could drink; if you put straw into the cattle pens so the cattle wouldn't freeze, then what about us? What could we ingest to keep our systems thawed out? What could we add to our bloodlines so we didn't freeze? That was our thinking. *Ya...what about us?!*

I drank some whiskey, too, the first time this young fellow found it, and my conscience bothered me so bad that I decided to never do that again. Not so with the other young thief. This dude was fast-tracking on the road to compromise, because he told me how he would take a couple of big shots a couple of times a week, and how shortly afterward he was hardly able to walk. "Frank will never miss it if I only take a couple of swigs a week," he said. "He'll think he drank it all himself!"

I remember thinking, *"Man, oh man, this kid is brave and all grown up! He knows what it feels like to be slightly drunk!*

Lo and behold, the very next day, Frank said to me, "Some little bastard is stealing my whiskey, right out of my private bedroom! Is it you Sammy?"

"I only took one swig and that was a while ago," I assured him.

"Well it's been going on for a couple of weeks now but I'm having my own fun with it!" Frank grinned. "I run behind the heifers when they're urinating and collect some of the juices to replenish my dwindling whiskey!"

I didn't know whether to laugh or cry when the young thief started bragging to me again of how he snuck into the hired man's trailer house and took a few swigs. It was now stored under some clothes so he had to look for it.

Think about this? How terrible is it? Who raised these reprobates anyway?

I never squealed on Mr. Frank in any way, but I did ask the kid, "Hey dude, what does the hired man's whiskey still taste like? Are you drinking a lot of it these days?"

He turned his nose up a little and told me it was a different bottle than it was the last time. It was definitely not as tasty as the first two kinds. He explained that the first bottle was a Johnny Walker brand. "Damn it was good! But this last bottle was the shits! Wish he'd stick to one kind. You know Sammy…the last bottle looked just like it came from a medicine cabinet. It's crazy but I'm not really sure what it was because the last few times it made me feel kinda sick. Tasted like a cross between alcohol and horse piss!"

To this day I wonder how he knew what that tasted like.

I've heard about the widow lady in the Bible who filled all those jars of clay from one bottle of oil that never ran dry.[2] But in this case, I saw for myself how a whiskey bottle became bottomless.

---

[2] (BibleGateway n.d.)

I sent this story to a friend who knew about this event, and he said the late Frank had told him that he fabricated the story about running behind the heifer. That would take too much effort and be dangerous besides. He just pissed in the bottle himself and got it over with.

So much for *"precious memories,"* ey?

STRAINING AT A GNAT

My uncle couldn't swallow a tiny pill on his first attempt, no matter how hard he tried, even if his life depended on it! He would get some honey on a spoon and put a little dab on the tip of his longest finger, then he would stick the little pill into the honey. He took a few deep breaths, planted his feet wide apart for balance, and proceeded to ram that little red pill down his esophagus as far as his index finger could possibly plunge it. He would be in a standing position with his head tilted way back, taking great gulps of water from the entire quart he was holding in his left hand. Finally, after what seemed like a drowning effort, he would slowly tilt his head into a normal position, explore the inside of his mouth with his tongue and try a few more dry swallows with his Adam's apple jerking up and down. Suddenly, he would get a bewildered look on his face, stick that long, wrinkled, crooked finger way back down in the recesses of his throat, and fish out that elusive little pill. It was half the original size, no bigger than a pinhead! I can still see him going half cross-eyed, staring at that little pill on his fingertip. There was always such a defeated look on poor Uncle's face.

He usually made a few more unsuccessful attempts. So what do you think he did next? He grabbed a big white marshmallow, jammed the pill into the middle of it, and without even any water or any effort that pill slid down that old, almost worn-out esophagus, past his Adam's apple like a rocket sled on wheels! Boom! Wham! Plop! The big white marshmallow, impregnated with the little red pill, hit the bottom of the digesting lagoon.

He looked over at me, the lone, fascinated spectator, and acted like everything was back to normal! He hadn't noticed that I was frantically scanning the newspaper ads to see if the circus needed a new act like they've never seen before.

Some of us can take a handful of pills and swallow them without even thinking, but it's a real trial for others to get even one down. Some of us can drive across the big bridge and not even think that we're crossing water, but others are terrified and literally buy a house on the other side of a bridge so they never have to cross it.

A big, strong, tough dry-waller once told me he was afraid to drive across the bridge in Evansville and that he had to hire someone to drive him across. He sat in the back seat all slouched down with his eyes closed until they were over the bridge. No joke!

There's a famous highway called *"Going to the Sun"* about three hours south of where I grew up in southern Alberta. It is a narrow, dangerous road cut into the side of the mountains with sides so steep and so deep that you can *"spit a mile."* The views are absolutely magnificent, and sometimes you're literally above the clouds! Trouble is, the guard rails are not very high and it's a lot easier driving on the inside against the mountain than on the outside a couple of feet away from the edge.

I once knew this kid who was absolutely petrified to cross over, no matter how slow and carefully his dad drove. He would sit on the floor in the back, halfway under the seat, with his head buried in a huge feather pillow. Every time his dad would go around a curve or make a tiny turn he would bleat, *"Daaaady...not so fast...Daaadddyyyy! Slow down...!"* Sounded just like a sick sheep!

Guess I'll never forget it because that kid was me. And they never let me live it down! Instead of sitting up and enjoying the view, I let my fear get the best of me, but later on, I was able to conquer that fear. I actually enjoy extreme heights...like flying in my plane.

You may be wondering what the lesson is in this swallowing episode. Like, why was he straining at the little red pill and swallowing a camel?

It's an old, old story from the beginning of time. It's so easy to do. We have one tiny little thing go wrong at the beginning of a perfectly gorgeous day, maybe one little word someone may have said that and they don't even realize how it offended us.

The birds are still singing, the trees are blooming, the garden is growing, we're alive and healthy. It's still a day like it was ordered by Heaven....BUT...*are we rejoicing?*

No! We're allowing that harmless incident to steal and ruin our perfectly beautiful day.

Many a bitter, unforgiving person carries a grudge for years that ends up destroying his entire life. It's insanity!

Counselors used to be able to tell if a person was missing a few marbles upstairs by giving them a simple test. They'd offer a chocolate bar with one hand and a hundred-dollar bill in the other hand. If he took the chocolate bar, they knew that he wasn't the sharpest knife in the drawer.

I know a mixed-up fellow who screamed at his wife for buying a trivial item at a garage sale when he himself had lost a fortune in the stock market.

Looking for a proper balance in life is so important, my friend. When I get upset about something I ask myself, *"Will it really matter in a year or ten years from now?"* If not, why get all bent out of shape?

My late father-in-law used to say, "Sammy, either you're a young man's slave, or an old man's darling." My own motto goes like this, "I'd much rather have a warm bed than win an argument."

What's that got to do with straining at a gnat? Everything.

Friendships, marriages, business partnerships, and all other human relationships rise and fall when we learn the art of graciousness. We need to make it a priority to focus on the good in other people instead of on the tiny little noises he or she makes cracking their gum in your ear or making loud chewing noises. Ha!

Every time I'm tempted to harshly judge an individual, the sweet Holy Spirit shows me things in my own life that quickly makes me change my attitude to graciousness instead.

The only people Jesus condemned were the self-righteous, religious folks. I absolutely love how he addressed them.

> *"But woe to you, scribes and Pharisees, hypocrites! For you shut up the kingdom of Heaven against men; for you neither go in yourselves, nor do you allow those who are entering to go in. Woe to you, scribes and Pharisees, hypocrites! For you devour widows' houses, and for a pretense make long prayers. Therefore you will receive greater condemnation. "Woe to you, scribes and Pharisees, hypocrites! For you travel land and sea to win one proselyte, and when he is won, you make him twice as much a son of hell as yourselves.*
>
> *"Woe to you, scribes and Pharisees, hypocrites! For you pay tithe of mint and anise and cumin, and have neglected the weightier matters of the law: justice and mercy and faith. These you ought to have done, without leaving the others undone. Blind guides, who strain out a gnat and swallow a camel! "Woe to you, scribes and Pharisees, hypocrites! For you cleanse the outside of the cup and dish, but inside they are*

full of extortion and self-indulgence. Blind Pharisee, first cleanse the inside of the cup and dish, that the outside of them may be clean also. "Woe to you, scribes and Pharisees, hypocrites! For you are like whitewashed tombs which indeed appear beautiful outwardly, but inside are full of dead men's bones and all uncleanness. Even so you also outwardly appear righteous to men, but inside you are full of hypocrisy and lawlessness.

"Therefore you are witnesses against yourselves that you are sons of those who murdered the prophets. Fill up, then, the measure of your fathers' guilt. Serpents, brood of vipers! How can you escape the condemnation of hell?
     ***Matthew 23:13-15, 23-28, 31-33** NKJV*

And what did Jesus say to the sinners?

"Neither do I condemn thee, go and sin no more!"
          ***John 8:11** KJV*

Wow, wow, wow, wow! What an awesome Friend!

SON OF A SEACOOK

TALK IS CHEAP

My late father said this many a time, "Talk is cheap. Whiskey costs money." He would say this to the salesmen that would find themselves at our door bragging about their products, how good they were, and what a great deal we would get on them. Dad would flash his best smile and say, "Talk is cheap. Whiskey costs money."

We would look to hire a new recruit, who would brag about himself and how good he was at doing everything, and my father, who was an excellent judge of character, would say to me, "You better let this one go, because talk is cheap. Whiskey costs money."

When I was younger, we did a lot of boxing, and I remember one fellow told me how badly he would lay a whipping on a friend of mine. I said to him, "I will be the one to tell whether or not you can lay a whipping on him!" Then I added Dad's famous words for good measure, "Talk is cheap. Whiskey costs money."

My dad and I

I remember the braggart's wife watching the fight as my friend was soundly thrashing her husband. She begged him to quit because even she could see he was receiving a whipping of a lifetime. The funny thing is, he kept taking more and more of a beating and ended up being a real sucker for punishment - maybe because those words were ringing in his ears; "Talk is cheap. Whiskey costs money."

One day my daughter sent me a link to a movie called *"Saving God,"* with TD Jakes. I thought about the title, *"Saving God."* Religion tells us many things about God and has raised grand expectations in people's lives, but nothing seems to happen as promised. People soon make excuses as to why things never happened, then go into this mode, which I have labeled "the saving God mode." I've said it over and over again that I'm not going to try to save God or try to prove His reality because God is big enough to take care of Himself!

One Sunday afternoon, when I was still living in Alberta, I was standing next to a gravel road, a mile away from our nearest neighbor. I used the road as a runway for my remote-controlled airplane and had just landed it when I looked up to see a man walking towards me. I realized he was a visitor from Belgium that was a friend of our neighbor. He had been in my home several days before when we held our in-home Bible study, and the first words out of his mouth on that beautiful day were, "Mr. Gary, I was listening to everything you said the other day, but I don't believe there is a God. Can you prove it to me?"

I looked at him and said, "Let me ask you a question. We're standing here on this beautiful, bright Sunday afternoon with the sun beating down and warming the earth. What you're asking me to do is light a candle so we can see the sun that is warming both of us. A man does not light a candle to see the sun! And neither will I try to prove the existence of God because He is big enough to take care of Himself! Why don't you ask God if He's real, and if He wants to, He can certainly show you."

He attempted several times to get me in an argument, but I never took the bait. He watched me fly the little airplane, and we made some small talk before he headed back to our neighbor's farm. An hour later, our neighbor called frantically, telling me their friend from Belgium was dead! He was only thirty-two years old. I asked my neighbor, who was a good friend of mine, what had happened. He told me he had come back from his walk to my place and walked over to the computer, where they had spent some time looking at topless women. He went into the bathroom, and a few minutes later, he started making these horrible noises, like some animal growling. The neighbor ran to the washroom to find this fellow down on all fours, walking in circles on his hands and knees, making these gruesome noises. Then he collapsed on the floor and died, just that fast!

> *I am He that liveth, and was dead; and, behold, I am alive forevermore, Amen; and have the keys of hell and of death.*
> **Revelation 1:18 (KJV)**

I built a feed mill in southern Alberta for a man whose brother had just won the 649 lottery. I was busy working on the feed mill when this lottery winning brother drove into the yard, came up to me, and said, "My brother tells me you're a great welder. Can you weld a broken spring for me? It's here on the back of my truck." I told him spring steel couldn't be welded because it will lose its spring when the weld overheats.

"Just weld it anyway," he said, hoisting it off the back. Because his brother employed me, I went against better knowledge and did the job, knowing full well that it wouldn't hold up.

"What do you think about Jesus?" I asked him as he was leaving.

"I don't have time for that," he retorted. "I'm in way too much of a hurry to talk about it now, anyway."

It was at the end of the workday, and it was time to go home for the evening, so I shut the welder down, closed all the valves to the oxygen-acetylene unit, and made sure things would be ready for the next day's work. This man headed south on the gravel road, and I went north on the same road. He got half a mile down the road where his son lived, right on the corner of an intersection, and plowed into a loaded gravel truck, sending him into eternity right in front of his son's house.

Talk Is Cheap - My Dad in his Prime

You may say that's absolutely terrible. It is! But what I remember is how he kept telling me to hurry, he had to go—continually asking me if I could hurry a little faster. I was trying to weld the big truck spring as best I could, and if you're a welder, you know what time that takes. I don't think we were together for more than fifteen minutes.

Back on our farm, we sold eggs to the public. Three young guys we knew dropped in to pick up a large carton of eggs and asked if they could pay later since they had to make it to a party and didn't want to be late. We knew them, so we agreed. They drove five miles east of our farm and ran head-on into a freight train, ending all three lives.

A young farmer once stopped in who was interested in buying a large generator that he wanted to hook up to his chicken barns as a backup during power outages. He had just lost thousands of chickens, and he was very discouraged, so I tried to give him a little bit of encouragement, urging him to turn to Jesus. He said he didn't believe any of that stuff and wasn't interested in talking about it. I sold him the generator, and he went home, picked up his twelve-year-old son, crossed an intersection, and was hit by a large truck. The boy had hardly a scratch, but the man was instantly killed. At his funeral, the preacher talked about how he was now with Jesus and how he loved God. I'm not putting him anywhere, but what the preacher said just wasn't true. Hopefully, folks won't have to lie about me at my funeral. Just saying.

I remember doing a concert in a little local restaurant and singing songs about Jesus. One old fellow was sitting in the back corner, and when I finished singing one of my songs, he said, "Hey Sammy! I'm going to shovel coal in hell!"

"My friend, you should never let such words come out of your mouth," I told him. He just chuckled harshly. Now, this is really sad and very crazy, but it's the truth. A month later, this man's son went off the road driving an oil tanker and was instantly killed. A month after that, the old-timer and his wife went on a fishing trip, and he died on the trip. So, my wife, my mom, and I went to visit the widow lady. We sat beside her and prayed with her. The ladies put shared warm hugs, and we invited her for Sunday dinner. She told us she would love to come and would see us Sunday morning. Friday night, we got the news that she was with some friends in a store and fell over dead. About a week later, their only daughter committed suicide. You may say, "This is insane. Why are you writing it?" I do have a point; trust me.

I recall visiting with my Cousin Philip who had moved from southern Alberta to Polson, Montana. We visited at my home over a cup of coffee for a couple of hours as he shared the Book of Psalms, Chapter One with me and my new bride. We had grown up together, and he knew me as well as I knew him. I thanked him for sharing with me and told him I was happy for him and the newfound joy he had in preaching the Kingdom. His last words to me were, "Cousin, you are not far from the Kingdom of God!"

Oka-a-a-a-y. Whatever he meant there, I wasn't too sure, but I believe I know today. Philip traveled back home to Montana, and I went back to my job, thinking about everything we had discussed. I was eighty-feet high, welding on an elevator leg when I looked down, and the fellow I was working for had just about reached me on the top level. "You're supposed to call home. One of your cousins who lives in Montana was just killed." What a great discussion we had just had the very last time we were together!

At Philip's funeral, I met his brother, who asked me when I would visit him; he hardly ever saw me. I don't remember my reply, but six months later, he was also killed in a logging accident.

Philip's wife's brother came to help her take care of the little children. Because my home in Alberta was a hub for young people, this young gentleman spent the weekend with us and did some fishing with another local boy. I talked to him about his life, and because he was a little older, I asked him if he was interested in girls. He said he was sure he would find the right one, but he was more interested in getting to know Jesus better at that moment (this was three months after Philip had been killed). He left our house and traveled back to Polson, Montana, and spent the day handing out gospel tracks and talking to people about Jesus. That evening he went swimming with a friend and drowned in a river with his newly-widowed sister looking on!

A friend and I took a trip to northern Idaho, and we dropped in to see one of my best friends. We stayed and visited for a couple of days. We had a meal together, and just before we left, I asked him if I could pray for him. He grinned and said, "You know Sam, I've always made fun of your zeal for the Lord, but you really have something. I want to pray for you, too, because God has used you to help me in my life."

"I would be honored, my friend, for you to pray for me," I told him. That date was September eleventh.

We drove home and went to a friend's house that evening for a little prayer meeting. We had put our prayer requests together, and I was kneeling at my chair when my phone rang. I heard my sweet wife tell me; "Your best friend and his brother just died when their airplane crashed." Life seems to be so unfair! Both of them had precious wives and beautiful children. Why, why, why?! I just don't know.

I once invited a hitchhiker home for dinner. He stayed in the community for the next eight years, lived in our basement for a time, drove an eighteen-wheeler with me, and became a real friend. He bought himself a new diesel pickup, put on nice wheels, and a new CB radio, which was hip in those days, and told me he was going back east to see his mother whom he hadn't seen for four years. I suggested that he wait a couple of days and keep driving the cattle truck until I was done with my job, then he'd be free to go. He looked at me and said, "Sam, I've got to leave in the morning, but could I come to your house and have your wife cut my hair and see your baby girl?"

My wife gave him a haircut while we visited. He went and stood by our new baby's crib and just gazed at her. He then turned around with a big grin on his face and said, "Is she ever cute! She's gonna look just like your beautiful wife. You know Sam, I've found what I'm looking for in Jesus. He has given me peace of mind, and all I want to do now is serve Him."

Early the next morning, I was driving the eighteen-wheeler, pulling a cattle trailer, and I heard, "Hey, Shotgun! I'll be seeing you when I get back!"

"Have a safe trip, buddy," I answered, and those were the last words I ever heard my buddy Elmer speak. Three hours from his home in Parry Sound, Ontario, he fell asleep, wandered into the path of an eighteen-wheeler, and died instantly. He was twenty-eight years old. His mother saw him in the box, but he never got to see his mother.

Back in my forties, I signed a five-year contract with Century Two Entertainment out of Nashville. We got an awesome five-piece band together, which we called the Sam Gary Band. In 2009, we found ourselves endorsed in the CMA country music magazine. Our genuinely fantastic lead guitar player and his lovely wife were staying at our place for the weekend, and we were discussing the possibilities of performing in the Cayman Islands. I looked at my friend and said, "We've been on the road awhile, and it's been a long time since I've had communion. Do you think you could serve us communion?"

"I would love to," he said.

"I'll run out to the motor home for a bottle of wine," his new bride offered.

My brother gave us each glass of wine and began, "As I think about having this communion, I see a table set in Heaven and a chair with my name on the plate..." A month later, on his thirty-second birthday, we laid him to rest. He had been speaking at the University of Texas and gathering shoes for the children of Haiti when he collapsed with an aneurysm and died. The last words I remember him saying to several of us men are these, "I have counted the cost. I have made my decision; I'm a follower of Jesus!"

I could go on and on telling you about people that I talked with while they were dying. Some of them died, saying they couldn't wait to see Jesus! One died claiming that he would never worship that imposter Jesus!

We can gather together every Sunday in our little places of worship, pat ourselves on the back, and console ourselves that we have the truth. We can condemn the sinner, preach hellfire, and try to make sure our theology is spot on. We can say countless words, but here in America, people are tired of just words! They want to see a manifestation of the Almighty, but this will never take place with us going through a dead religious ritual, trying to find people who agree with us so we can build our little elite groups.

Everywhere, every day, people are dying. Death is no respecter of persons—not the young, the middle-aged, and definitely not the old. Instead of pulling people into our closed, secluded, denominational circles, we need to be equipping people and reaching into all sectors of society and bringing the culture of Heaven back down to Earth by the love of Jesus in our hearts. This is our mandate, and it is illegal for us to run and hide and not take dominion because today is our day! Talk is still cheap, and whiskey still costs money.

Thanks, Dad, I haven't forgotten you and I never will! I'm looking forward to seeing you soon.

Your son, Sam Gary

SON OF A SEACOOK

SUPERNATURAL CONNECTION

The year was 1989, and I was thirty years old. My father had passed away in July of 1987 at the young age of fifty-eight, but before he died, he wrote me a letter and asked me to read it at his funeral.

Dad had grown up in the WW2 era and had seen a lot of drama in his short life. I often told him, "Dad, you have experienced religion but what you need is Jesus! Religion crucified Jesus and religion always hurts people and leaves them empty, let-down, and forsaken."

I could write a small book about my dad. Yes, he was just a man, but I knew him well and several outstanding traits of his keep popping into my mind. When we were a young family at home, Dad watched over us like a hen watches her baby chicks. He had the reputation with the other youth and parents that he would not tolerate his daughters staying out too late, seldom for sleepovers anywhere, and never unchaperoned. One time when all us young people were eating at the Pizza Hut for someone's birthday, the phone rang. Instantly some wise guy pipes up, "That's Uncle Sammy, looking for his girls!"

Dad hated gossip. He was never one to sit around and "shoot the breeze" so to speak. I never, ever heard him tell a lie, not even a little one. He never told off-colored jokes or laughed at them either. And there wasn't a false bone in his body! What you saw was what you got! He was a man of few words, a loyal heart, and genuine integrity.

In the last years of Dad's life, he worked on my construction crew, building huge grain handling systems that loaded train cars. Subsequently, we often parked alongside the railroad tracks in these small prairie towns. Some of our jobs would take us months to finish and some would take over a year.

I owned a large crane which Dad operated, lifting supplies to us as we worked way up on the elevator. Dad made a basket out of some heavy-duty left-over black belting that we could sit in and be lifted off the top of the buildings. This was way faster than climbing hundreds of stairs to the ground for our coffee breaks or whatever else we had to do.

This worked well for a long time and really shortened the time it took us to get down. Then one fine day, Dad was lifting me off of the elevator from ninety feet in the air when suddenly I dropped about ten feet before I was jerked to a neck-jolting stop. I glanced at the belt and realized there was a mere quarter-inch of it left holding me up in the air! I would have fallen to my death, or have been severally crippled if the belt had severed totally. Dad must have had his thoughts somewhere else when he took his foot off the clutch brake, then he realized what happened and slammed it down again, tearing the thick, commercial belt almost to the point of breaking.

He slowly and carefully let me the rest of the way down, examined the tear in the belt, and said, "Son, don't tell your mother."

Let me tell the world that after he made the next basket, nothing could have torn it apart!

We were working in Looseland, Saskatchewan, building an elevator for Pioneer Grain when my father had a massive heart attack. The doctors said that he'd be gone by morning, but he lived another six weeks, during which he had a life-transforming experience with Jesus and found the peace he had been searching for all his life.

One of the first things Dad said to me after his heart attack was, "Thanks for not giving up on me, Son...and thanks for preaching Jesus."

After his experience with Christ, he wouldn't let anyone around him speak ill of others, but he'd sit in the rocking chair praying for his family and friends, and for all the folks around him.

My sister and I were with Dad the night he died, and we talked with him until he was gone. I asked him if he was afraid to go, and he said, "I'm ready to meet Jesus, Son."

The nurse on duty that night kept asking my sister and I if we were alright, and I told her, "I've never been better because my dad has gone to meet Jesus! No more pain, no more needles, no more heart surgeries, and no more religious drama! He's well taken care of now."

"I've never seen anything quite like this," she said, "and I just wanted to make sure you were both okay."

A couple of months later, I came upon a stalled vehicle and a man walking, so I stopped and picked him up to haul him to a gas station. We had a little time, so I told him my Dad's experience; how he had come to Jesus, and how we were with him when he died. The man looked at me and said, "I know what you're saying is true because my wife was on duty that night and she told me all about it."

Wow!

A little later a man from Ohio called and asked me if I would be willing to fly back East and share this testimony in their churches, one in Ohio, one in Pennsylvania, and one in Florida. So away I went!

During the short hop from Akron-Canton to O'Hare, Chicago, I remember getting on the plane. As the doors were closing, I just whispered a short little prayer that went something like this, "Lord…it's easy for me to visit with people but if You want me to talk with someone, please let them ask questions so I will know You're involved in what I'm doing."

Just before the plane took off, a fine gentleman sat down beside me, got all comfortable, looked at me, and said, "Young man, where are you heading tonight?"

"I'm going back East," I replied,

"Well, what are you doing back there?"

"Do you really want to know?" I asked him.

"Sure I do. We've got some time," he replied.

So I shared what I was planning to do. "You'd get along well with my son-in-law," he told me. "He's into all this Jesus stuff too."

"Where are you going?" I asked.

"I work for the military and I'm going to a place you've probably never heard of in southern California."

"Try me." I said. "My brother-in-law's dad is a military officer in southern California."

"I'm headed for Ridgecrest," He informed me.

"Ridgecrest! Who exactly are you going to see?"

He told me he was meeting up with my brother-in-law's dad!

"Sir!" I said. "There are seven billion people in this world and you are going to meet my brother-in-law's father! This is not an accident! I prayed for an encounter with God and now I met you of all people! Do you care to read the letter my dad wrote before he passed away? Or the letter I'm carrying from a doctor in Toronto about people that are ready to die?"

"Yes, I'll read them," he agreed. "But what about people that are about to die?"

"This doctor said if anyone doesn't believe in the hereafter they should come to visit his hospital and listen to some of the people they resuscitate. They start screaming for him to not let them die because they're going to a devil's hell and they haven't had time for Jesus."

He took the letters slowly and read them both. "This is some pretty heavy material," he said, looking at me soberly.

"It sure is," I agreed. "Any of us can die any time and we need to be in right standing with God by believing in His Son, Jesus."

I had no sooner spoken than a woman behind us stood up and sunk her prefab fingernails into my shoulder, screaming for help. "My husband isn't breathing…he's dying…!"

The stewardesses rushed to help and performed CPR on the man until his heart started beating again and he regained consciousness. But the fine military gentleman came unglued.

"God brought me here!" He stated. "I've got all the things in life that some men can only dream about! I've got money, an awesome career, and a family but I'm not ready to die. How do I find peace with God?"

Later, my brother-in-law's father called from Ridgecrest and told me he had heard all about the plane ride.

Wow! Just wow!

God…You're so-o-o-o indescribably awesome! What else makes sense besides serving You?

And Dad, I can't wait to see you again! There's so much I want to tell you. So much.

BULLS & HEIFERS

The year was 1975, and I was seventeen years old. We were living in southern Alberta, Canada, at the time. One of my cousins married a fellow named Nevin from North Carolina, a very positive influence in our youth group's lives. He loved to encourage us, go camping with us in the Rockies, and teach us how to sing in four-part harmony.

One day, he got a dangerous brain wave and asked a bunch of us young men if we'd like to climb Crow's Nest Mountain back in Crow's Nest Pass. Always ready for adventure, six of us young men, some married and some single, our young minister Roman, and my Uncle Paul signed up with Nevin to tackle the mountain.

We had our lunches packed by the anxious women while listening to all the warnings why we shouldn't attempt the climb, then retired early to bed so that we could leave by 4:00 A.M.. Nevin figured he had the day pretty well calculated - we would leave promptly at four, drive eighty miles to the pass, get as close to the base of the mountain as we could, and be above the tree line by 8:00 A.M. or 9:00 A.M. for sure.

This majestic mountain stands in a wild place, inhabited by grizzlies, mountain lions, and other dangerous wildlife. Looking back today, I realize that despite the predators, we were our own worst enemies by far. The mountain was about 9,500 feet tall with sheer rock walls that rose 400 to 600 feet at a time!

Sometimes we would be on a foot-wide ledge with the valley dropping thousands of feet below us. We climbed without ropes, and at one point, we found ourselves stuck at a place that was impossible to scale. There was a sheer wall ahead of us with no way of backtracking. Someone came up with the bright idea of tying all our coats together by the sleeves, which we did. Then we tied them on to the bravest among us, and he scaled the vertical wall, secured himself, and helped the rest of us up the coat-line. By some incredible miracle, we all made it! Around noon, we reached the summit, and what a spectacular view it was! You could literally see 100 miles in every direction out onto the flatlands of the prairie. Uncle Paul had decided he was too old to climb the rock walls, so he said he'd wait for us above the tree line until we came back down.

Crow's Nest

My Uncle Paul was a wonderful, kind man who always had a big smile on his face. I think he was one of my favorite uncles because I could relate to him easily. In his later years, the ministry ordained him, and he always tried hard to do what was right. During harvest, Uncle Paul asked me to drive a combine for him because he was a little behind. The field was out on the Indian reservation, where he leased land together with his brother and his family. We left early Monday morning, drove out to the reservation, worked all day and half the night, and crashed in the bunkhouse. My double cousin was on the crew, and every morning before breakfast, my Uncle Paul would watch us wash our hands at the washbasin. If we didn't use enough soap, he'd make us do it again. He said he had a weak stomach and a vivid imagination, so he had to make sure we were spotless when eating at his table. The bathroom on the reservation was an old wooden outhouse, and every time we'd use it, he'd follow us to the basin and make us wash. All this took place long before COVID!

I know it was wrong, and we probably shouldn't have done it, but one night Uncle was using the outhouse, and Cousin and I snuck down to have some fun. He grabbed one side, and I grabbed the other, and we started rocking it as hard as we could while making sure it never completely toppled. The German slang and the horrible threats that burst out of that outhouse from dear old Uncle would have made all his parishioners blush. We laughed so hard that we could hardly run and hide, and we didn't dare show our faces for quite some time.

But I guess Uncle had it coming. Cousin Philip told me that he was running a swather one black, moonless night when Uncle Paul stealthily climbed up the back of the machine and screamed as he grabbed him. Phil said he whirled the machine around in total terror, and Uncle Paul went flying off the back. Then he chased him with the swather, long after he knew who it was. Good thing he didn't run him over.

Another night, one of my girl cousins ran a combine in the same field I was in, and I blinked my lights for her to stop because I had a coke and chips I wanted to give her. Every other night, I enjoyed a wine-dipped cigar, and this was one of those evenings. I had just put that ol' cigar in my mouth to take a deep drag when this hairy hand shot out of nowhere and pulled the cigar right out of my mouth. Uncle exclaimed, "Hahahaha! I caught you in the act!" He was grinning like a possum eating crap. He had actually climbed up the back of the combine, over the running motor, and through the grain hopper so he could reach through the cab window without being seen! He must have been desperate to get his hands on that cigar!

Anyway, Uncle was a blast, and this particular day he was waiting patiently just above the tree line on Crow's Nest mountain. When it was time to descend, we thought maybe we should send a couple of the bravest climbers down to hire a chopper to pick the rest of us off. In the end, we soberly told each other that we love each other just in case something happened, then together we started our terribly dangerous descent. Finally, we staggered off the rock wall, and there, patiently waiting, was dear old Uncle Paul. He said he thought of going through the trees back to the truck, but was afraid of the grizzlies. To this day, I find it hard to believe that everyone got down safe. Later on, we found out it was very illegal to climb without ropes.

Now on Crow's Nest Mountain, an unfortunate few get eaten by bears every year. Ignorant folks would come from back east and hike in our mountains with bells on their runners, thinking this would deter a big old grizzly. How very wrong they were! When you find bear poop, you dig through it with a stick to see if you can spot some little bells or pieces of Nike runners floating around. We had a fellow from our local town who guided people through the grizzly territory for sixteen years, but the grizzlies got him one day. It's no joke, folks! Bear spray and little kitty-cat bells don't stop a thousand-pound griz!

Well, back to my story. We got back into town at the foot of the mountain, and Uncle said, "Boys, we've gotta find a washroom!" We pulled up to a little restaurant, and all jumped out, trying to dash for the washroom with Uncle hurrying along. "Boys," he said, "you need to have some respect for me because I'm older. Let me use the washroom first." So we did. He went up to the two doors. One was marked BULLS, and the other HEIFERS. Uncle turned around and said, "I'm not a bull, and I'll never go in there!" pointing to the HEIFER bathroom.

To this day, I don't know what poor Uncle did, but five of us boys dashed for the BULL room. We were all quite desperate, and no one was going to wait. I made it to the pot first and didn't even bother to raise the ring. One cousin used the sink, the other one the urinal, and the other used the sink on the opposite side. Without warning, a stranger stepped into the room. The two cousins at the sinks on either side of me coolly redirected their aim to the pot where I was standing. We started to laugh uncontrollably as it sprayed all over the ring, the floor, and my blue jeans. It's impossible to have a good aim when you're shaking with laughter.

The stranger shot us a startled glance and exited faster than he had come in. I still don't know where Uncle disappeared to, but I know for sure it wasn't into the BULL room.

SON OF A SEACOOK

A HOUSE FULL OF LADIES

I still remember the day and the setting. It was blisteringly hot, and my father and I were changing the shovels on an old, thirty-six-foot International cultivator in front of our welding shop. Not a breeze was stirring, and we were sweating through our shirts. Lying in the shade underneath the tractor nearby was my faithful blue heeler, Jack. He was my constant companion, and just then, he was watching us work.

No one tied up in the dogs on our farm. It was a dog's paradise, big and roomy with miles of acres to explore. Our neighbor man, however, kept his dogs tied to the fuel tank so no-one could steal his petrol. This made his dogs very vicious, and when he did let them run, they would slink along Highway 52 and chase cars. You really wouldn't want to meet them in the dark!

We knew three goofy young fellows who would sometimes drive slowly past the farm with the truck's end-gate open, just baiting the dogs to chase them. Of course, the dogs came snarling out, trying to bite the tires, and they would let them have it with a shotgun. It didn't take the dogs long to figure it out. When there was a gun in sight, they hid.

Now, these three fellows completely lacked any common sense between their ears, so what did those lunatics do? They drove by the poor farmer's yard in the middle of the night with a shotgun and took potshots at the dogs guarding the tank in front of the house. In my book, these fellows should be in jail.

When our children were young, we had this beautiful black and white Husky that they loved and played with constantly. The dog was a fierce protector yet very gentle with the children. One summer day, a man came by our house and shot the dog who was cavorting in the field right in front of our house. It broke my children's hearts—what a bunch of monsters.

Well, back to my main story, which happened when my four sisters and I were much younger. Our house was situated alone on a hill where you could see the rest of the farm buildings. The canal, where we would swim all summer, ran right through the middle, and Highway 52 split the place in half. You could see the houses where five other families lived, the welding shop, the chicken barns, and the grain bins on the south side of the road. On the north side was the big, gray barn, complete with a fabulous hayloft, where a thousand memories were made. It boasted a long rope hung from the ceiling where us kids could swing the entire width of the loft, and to someone like me, who was just three feet tall, it was amazing. There were cows, horses, pigs, and steers, which added to the spice of farm life.

Our kitchen had a great big picture window, which was the only screen we had while growing up. You could watch real live weather as it approached from many miles away, and you could watch a lot of activity on the farm. Sometimes Dad used this big window to his advantage while we ate our meals. If I had a choice morsel on my plate, he would act like he was interested in something outside and mutter a few words under his breath. Of course, I craned my neck to see what was going on outside, and he would take the opportunity to steal the last piece of bacon from my plate. Ha, ha!

So back to the work at the welding shop. Dad and I had finished part of the job, and we were walking up to the house for lunch when we spied three people walking along the highway. "I'm going to see who they are," I told Dad. "Maybe they need a good meal." I went flying down across the bridge and over the canal and yelled at the three hitchhikers to come on over. After asking where they were from and where they were headed, we found out they were from southern Ontario, and the only destination they had was going out west! *(Go west, young man. Go west!)*

They graciously accepted my offer to come for lunch, so we spent the noon hour becoming acquainted with three complete strangers. One of them, Amos, had a bad limp. Another one, Scott, had a glass eye, and the third one, Bubba, was short and chubby.

Just thinking about this interesting Bubba fellow opens a whole new chapter. He and Amos ended up staying for a couple of years and helping on the farm, and Scott ended up drifting on. Etched in my memory is the day when no one could find the keys for one of our much-needed farm trucks. Back then, everyone left their keys in their vehicles and didn't worry about them being stolen because everybody knew everybody else in the community. Maybe a neighbor needed to borrow it for some reason. As a general rule, we trusted each other.

After searching for the keys for a couple of hours, I asked Bubba if he knew where they were. I can still see him sheepishly looking down as he slowly pulled them out of his pocket. He told me he was just making sure he had a vehicle for the evening to go fishing! There he was, a new employee, taking the keys out of a truck that wasn't his. This didn't go down well with anyone, and I told Bubba it was totally unacceptable. He got all choked up and said he was gonna work for the neighboring farmer. Away he went, but two weeks later he came back, asking for his old job.

"Hey, Bubba. What happened at the neighbors? How come your job didn't last?" He got this stupid grin on his face and went on to explain. After working hard with the hogs all day, Bubba's employer went to the house and filled his master bathroom tub with hot, sudsy water. The tired man was planning a long, relaxing, de-stinking bath. But get this! Guess who beat him into his own private bathtub? You're right; it was Bubba, sitting in water so deep that just his nose and his toes stuck out. And scattered beside the gleaming tub lay all of Bubba's dirty clothes. You guessed it. Bubba was choked that the farmer yelled at him to get the hell off his place. Yes, it was another strange place, another strange house, another strange man and woman, but he, Bubba, beat them into their own bathtub! When the good Lord handed out brains, Bubba thought He said trains and waved them on by!

I wondered then, and I still wonder; who raised these kids? What were their parents like? How did they relate to others? I remember telling Bubba about this pretty girl who used to babysit the neighbor's rowdy kids. Right off the bat, Bubba said he'd like to meet her. *Uh oh! Now what?* We happened to be driving past the place where the young girl was babysitting. Bubba said he wanted to stop and introduce himself to her. I told him he was crazy and that he didn't have a chance with her, but I stopped anyway. He got out of the truck, went over to the front door, squatted down below the window sill, and knocked on the door.

I can still see her coming to the window and looking at our truck parked in her driveway, and wondering who knocked. Bubba put the bill of his cap up in the air, made a stupid face, and stood up a foot away from the girl, who was on the other side of the glass. She gave a scream and hurried back into the house. He came over with a dumb grin on his face and said, "Ya, she sure is cute."

My friend and I decided to teach Bubba a few manners, or maybe a few good lessons. So, we stopped at the pharmacy for a few special ingredients. We mixed a bag of Smarties™ with a box of Ex-Lax™ and set it in plain sight. Sure enough, old Bubba just started munching down on our goodies as fast and as hard as he could without even asking! It was so-o-o predictable that a child could have forecasted it. Our plan was to clean up Bubba inside, then work on his outside.

Bubba kept munching the bag all by himself and proceeded to tell us that some of the Smarties™ weren't quite as sweet as the others. We burst out laughing, and old Bubba got really frustrated; we wouldn't tell him why. Let me tell you; he was sure about to find out. And if you don't know what was so funny, buy yourself some Ex-Lax™—they're really tasty!

Bubba had bought some expensive lotion because of a rash he had all over his body. This was forty years ago, but the lotion still cost him around twenty-five dollars, which is equivalent to about 100 dollars today. We convinced him that that lotion was not what he needed and that he should exchange the lotion for mascara. I can still see that poor lady behind the counter. She could not stop laughing as Bubba persistently tried to convince her that he needed mascara instead of the lotion.

Now that Bubba wasn't the trickster, but ended up being the brunt of the joke, things weren't quite as funny! Bubba, if you can't take it, then don't hand it out, either. Our time with Bubba soon came to an end as one bad decision after another took him on a fast road downhill. I found out the expensive way that you can only help someone who truly wants to help themselves. Amos stayed around for eight years. You say, "Really?" Yes, he lived in our basement, ate at our table, bathed in our tub, worked on our farm, came to our church, chased our girls, became the brunt of our jokes, and became family.

Amos was raised a "horse and buggy Mennonite." His left foot pointed straight ahead when he walked, but his right foot jutted out at a 45° angle, causing a very unique way of walking. He was training a horse to hitch to a buggy when the horse took off. Somehow his foot got caught between the spokes of the buggy wheel, and his leg got broken. Amos liked girls the same as any other red-blooded young fellow, and by and by, he moved out of our cool, damp basement to live in much greener pastures. In fact, he moved into my uncle's house, and my uncle had six beautiful daughters!

Well, well! It's just occurring to me how Amos's emotions must have rocked! He was moving out of a cold, dark, damp basement with concrete walls all around him into a house decorated with flowers, dresses, beautiful brown eyes, and beautiful smells. This would arouse any man's sleeping senses, make his lonely heart race, and quicken his drowsy mind unless, of course, he was a eunuch.

Yes, I finally understand. Poor Amos was completely and totally overcome. The change was just too steep, or should I say, drastic? The incline should have been gradual, not completely horizontal, like hitting a concrete wall. What was I thinking? Was I not considering my friend's emotional well-being? Was I not being sensitive to the things in life that really matter? Feelings, feelings, feelings!

Yes, yes. Maybe Amos should have graduated from my basement to a room upstairs in the main house, then maybe lived a little while with the other hired man. *Then* we could have moved him into this environment with all the beautiful sights and sounds and smells. Poor bedazzled Amos moved right in with Uncle and his beautiful daughters. Immediately, without asking me, you, or anyone else, what did he do? He asked the oldest daughter out for a date. Well, she said no. So, a couple of days later (no, no, NO Amos!), he asked the second oldest sister out. She also gave him a big fat no. What did the poor guy do? He went and asked the third sister if she would be his girlfriend. Well, to make a short story shorter, the third young lady also said no.

Poor Amos hit the floor! He bit the dust! He went back to the basement. Figuratively speaking, he didn't want to live anymore. He played the dating stock market and lost his first three options. Yes, he told me he was done; he just wanted to be with Jesus. Sometimes a broken heart hurts worse than death. I've been to a lot of funerals where I couldn't make myself cry, and it has made me feel guilty because when one of my beloved dogs is at the end of his life, I hurt way worse than I did when some of my acquaintances died. I think I know why! I believe it's because I trusted my dog, had a relationship with him, and understood him.

I told Amos, "You need to get yourself together, get your heart off the floor, grab the bull by the horns, and stand up like a man! Furthermore, I can help you a little bit if you want to know the truth about why you missed three in a row. An available, eligible, kitchen-locked, house-prisoned damsel in distress is looking for some tall, dark, handsome stranger to swoop in, knock her off her feet, and rescue her, with her heart beating so fast she's blushing crimson red at the sight of him. She's not looking for some hired man to arrive in one day and ask her and two more of her siblings for a date in just one month? Before they even know who he is or where he's going, and where he came from? Ya? What ya thinking, buddy?"

I guess he wasn't...

I said, "The very fact that you asked these girls out in such close succession shows that you're just after a girlfriend. In fact, any girl will do. That doesn't enhance anyone of the ladies' feelings of being someone special, or of being someone's one and only."

"Well," he told me, "I am just very lonely, and I'm looking for a friend." I told him that I understand, that I would be with him all the way, and I just dropped the subject.

Amos and I did a lot of grain and cattle hauling together. On one trip, I was resting in the passenger seat, and I looked over at Amos behind the steering wheel. I'm sure you've seen this too; the person is awake, their eyes are open, but no one's at home. I could see he was clearly in dreamland. I said his name softly, and he never responded. I said his name a little louder, still no response. He was driving our big rig, hauling eighty thousand pounds of nitrate, and was in another world. Maybe he was thinking about the three girls he had asked out, or maybe he wasn't, but one thing I know, when I let out a high-pitched scream, he came to his senses really fast. I told him he was responsible for a lot of lives. If he was tired, he needed to tell me, and I would take over the driving.

He said, "Sometimes a man's mind just wanders, and I forget what I'm doing." I didn't like it. I've taught a few guys how to run an eighteen-wheeler, and I'm a very, very fussy driver. It's hard for me to crawl into the sleeper of the truck if I have the slightest worry about the driver behind the wheel. A friend of mine in Pennsylvania fell asleep behind the wheel and killed a bunch of people, and crippled some people that were in his vehicle. This is so unacceptable. If you're getting tired, pull over, get out and let someone else drive.

It's no different than pointing a loaded gun at people and pulling the trigger every now and then and hoping nobody gets hurt. I have no tolerance for people who drive sleepy behind the wheel. Amos stayed in Alberta for about eight years, and one day during spring seeding, he said to me, "Sammy, I haven't seen my mother for years, and my heart aches for her."

I replied, "If you drive the truck one more week 'til we're finished seeding, I'll take over your job."

"No, I'm leaving tomorrow," he insisted. "I need to see my mother."

"If you have to go, you have to go," I agreed. "I see my mother every day."

So, we went to town, and he bought himself brand-new tires and rims for his new Chevy diesel pickup truck. He also installed a brand-new CB radio. He came to our house the night before he left for Ontario and asked my wife to give him a haircut and take a few pictures of him. We had just brought our first baby girl home from the hospital, so I asked if he wanted to see the baby. I can still see him standing there, looking down at our precious little Jessica. "I'm leaving early in the morning," he said. "I'll see you when I get back. There's one more thing I'd like to tell you before I go. All that matters to me is if I am pleasing to God. I don't care if the girls don't like me or how things go, but it does matter if I have peace with God. I've found what I'm looking for, Sammy."

"That's wonderful! I'm so happy for you!" I told him.

The next morning, I hauled a load of cattle for the slaughterhouse, and I talked with Amos on his new CB radio 'til he faded into the distance and was too far away to connect. Amos drove to Ontario, and three hours from his home in Elmira, he fell asleep and had a head-on collision with an oncoming eighteen-wheeler. That was the end of the road for Amos. He never did get to see his mother.

We were always playing friendly jokes on each other during the time we worked together, just to add some spice to life. In the end, Amos tricked me good and had the last laugh! The coffin they buried him in was an ultra-heavy homemade job, and I was one of his pallbearers even though I had just had surgery on my shoulder. I was a foot taller than the other pallbearers, and with my newly-operated shoulder, I carried the entire weight of my side the whole 200 yards to the graveside. You got me, my friend! R.I.P!

What's the point of my story? You never know what a little act of kindness will do. Inviting someone in for a meal or going the extra mile can change a life. I have a lot more memories of my friend Amos. I would get him laughing while trying to stay sober, and he would dissolve in fits of coughing and gagging because he was laughing so hard.

Many times I became impatient with him when we drove a truck together. I would be done with my meal, and he would just be salting his. Ha! And now, forty years later, what does it really matter if he was slow, if he was different? All that matters is that somebody took the time to make his life more enjoyable.

Everywhere I go, I see "Amoses." Folks who are just a little different and don't fit in with what we call normal. They're not great at sports or much of anything; they're just people who give you the opportunity to love on them.

Don't miss the opportunity! It's an investment that pays forever.

DESPERATE CIRCUMSTANCES

Back in the late eighties and into the nineties, we built a lot of grain handling systems along the railroad tracks on the vast prairies of Alberta, where I spent the first 42 years of my life. My company was called "Roman Builders" after a friend of mine, which is another story in itself. *Haha!*

We were setting up a grain elevator in the windy city of Lethbridge, and the folks who were running the elevator had a one-track mind as they produced and marketed flour all across North America. They had to think about making flour at some time or another in order to do the job, but it seemed that all they ever talked about was sex, and it sure wasn't from a Sunday School perspective. They had all kinds of sexual paintings scribbled on the wall, and I remember thinking how truly unbelievable it was that men could be on the same level as an animal. I guess if you believe you're an animal, why not act like one, was my logical conclusion.

So, while working in this environment, we would bring gospel tracks to this workplace and put them where folks can readily pick them up. What did they do? They made sure I watched them pick up a tract, then went to the garbage and dropped it in. Then they slapped their hands together, looked at me defiantly, and nodded their heads. They were telling me, *"Mr. Sam, keep your organic, healthy-minded food to yourself. We've been eating crap for so long that we actually enjoy it, and now it's all we want."*

It's the same shock you get when you've learned to eat healthy, and you see a dear soul pushing a shopping cart at Walmart, full of chips, pop, chocolate bars, and breakfast twinkies! It takes the human body twenty-four hours to turn good food into waste, but these pour souls were eating crap to begin with! Anyway, no charge for that health lesson.

Well, at this job-site was a fellow who I discovered was a silent professor of Christ. He sort of cozied up to me and said he was helpless and couldn't do much about all the graffiti, but after a couple of weeks of working with him, I saw him tear some of the hardcore pictures down. I approached the one fellow who had a bunch of naked women on the wall and asked him if the pictures were his wife and daughters. He instantly turned violent and tried to intimidate me. So, I asked him if he didn't realize that they were someone's daughters, someone who had not taught them or protected them, or schooled them in the art of being a virtuous woman and not just a piece of naked flesh on a wall for some perverted old man to lust after. He admitted that it never entered his mind.

Another time, I took my seven-year-old son with me to a place of business that our company supported heavily. The boss had just hung a picture of someone's naked daughter up on the wall, and my little boy caught sight of it. I quickly turned him around, and I said, "Sir, I appreciate you as a businessman, but if you leave someone's naked daughter hanging on your wall, I will never again spend a dollar here. What you do in your own home is none of my business, but what you do here certainly is!" The man tore it down on the spot.

How about you? Do you think it's okay to put someone's naked daughter up on a wall poster? How about when they sell someone's daughter for sex trafficking? At what point will you stand up and say that it's *NOT OKAY?!*

Desperate Circumstances

Now back to the flour mill saga. The man who was a professing Christian said he'd like me to meet his son because he could sure use some good influence in his life. I told him I'd love to meet him; the sooner, the better. God is always at work with His people behind the scenes! When we don't get what we ask for immediately, we need to remember this little secret.

Every day I saw people throwing our gospel tracts into the trash, and every night, unknown to me, the professing Christian's son was sweeping down the mill. He would tip over the trash can, fish out the tracts, and read them. After I got to know him, he said he looked forward to emptying the trash cans! Haha, devil! The Lord rebuke you!

I love to play guitar, and one weekend I was pickin' away when this particular professing Christian came to mind over and over. The strangest thought kept coming to my mind, *"Take your guitar to his home and play some tunes for him."* I didn't really want to, but I just couldn't shake the prompting, so-o-o I called my brother-in-law and asked him to come along, and away we went.

We knocked on the door, guitar in hand, and the gentleman and his wife came to the door. "Would you like to hear a couple of tunes?" I asked.

"Come in, come in!" they responded. We sat down on chairs, self-invited guests at a man's place that we barely knew, and started singing songs that we DID know. Talk about feeling awkward. It felt like we were imposing on these people. We had a cup of tea, sang a few more songs, and said good-bye.

I found out later what happened that fateful evening. Behind a door in one of the bedrooms was a young man sitting with the end of his rifle in his mouth. Before he pulled the trigger, he said, "God.

If You are real, speak to me." He put the gun in his mouth, and just as he started to pull the trigger, he heard someone singing and playing guitar in the living room. He slowly removed the rifle from his mouth and shuddered with the realization of what he had just about done. This young man went on to be an outstanding citizen, a good father, and a witness of God's awesome grace. He and I started a halfway house, which is another story.

In a nutshell, we were stolen blind, and our credit cards were used in distant cities as we tried to believe in a bunch of users who didn't even believe in themselves. My policy today is; unless someone is willing to go halfway, you can't help them. And if you want permanent social distancing, just borrow a friend some money.

So, my dear reader, when you feel that strange unction, that pull on your spirit or that still, small voice tugging at your heart, listen up! Follow through and don't discard it as nothing. For as a child of God, not one hair falls from your head without our good, good Father knowing all about it. There's no such thing as chance in the life of God's children, and because He lives inside of us, we can hear from Him, and He will guide our steps in all areas of life.

BRIEFCASE

I have this dear old friend that I met about forty-six years ago. It takes a long time to make a real friend, but he was one of mine. He was an accomplished, successful man, at least in my opinion. For example, when the former Romanian president, Nicolae Ceausescu, was overthrown, my friend bought several tracts of land in Romania, just to see it inflate by 300 percent.

My friend had a heart for people. He had sacrificed years of time helping folks who had taken him for granted and taken advantage of his generous heart. But I'm getting ahead of myself.

After buying this land, my friend stayed in Romania for a while. He loved the Romanian people and tried to provide work for them. He located a group of people in Romania that were "good carpenters" and got them to start building grandfather clocks.

Unfortunately, Romanians grew up with communism and socialism, so they didn't know how to operate in a capitalistic society. I did a trade show with one of them in High Point, North Carolina and he would relate stories of his life in Romania, including how they survived under a dictatorship. He said they put scotch tape on a quarter and as they would talk on the phone, they would pull the quarter in and out of the payphone. This way, they could talk as long as they wanted for free! They would trick companies into paying them extra money for the cheese they delivered by filling a container in the back of the truck with water and then driving on the scale. After they drove off they would drain the water and since they were paid by the pound, they would make more money. This Romanian had more dirty tricks up his sleeve than Carter has liver pills, but he said he had to cheat for his family to survive in a morally and financially corrupt country.

So it's no surprise that they took advantage of my old friend. They were just living out their philosophy for survival. Whenever they faced the slightest roadblock they would unconsciously revert to their communistic way of thinking. Their thought patterns had been trained in a society where the government bankrupted the people's money. And when someone who genuinely loved them came along and tried to help, what did they do? Reverted back to default. We all become what we think. We are the victims or victors of our own thought processes.

Thoughts lead to emotions and feelings. Feelings determine our attitudes. Attitudes determine our actions. Actions determine our habits. Habits determine our lifestyle. That's why true change doesn't spring from New Year's resolutions or personal recommitments. It only comes by changing the original thought patterns of our inner man, or hard drive.

"For as a man thinketh in his heart, so is he."
Proverbs 23:7 KJV

A person could save themselves a lot of broken relationships and bad experiences if they could just decipher another parties' philosophy. Lots of times they wouldn't do business with them in the first place.

When the Romanians ran out of work they called my friend under a false name and gave him an order for 500 clocks. So he went ahead in good faith and built 500 clocks! That's where I come in.

One day my friend came to visit me in Alberta and pulled out these gorgeous pictures of grandfather clocks with the most intricate flowers engraved in the woodwork. I was walking around in circles, completely stunned, telling him these are the most beautiful things that I have ever seen. I asked, "What are you doing with them? How are you gonna sell 'em? Who's gonna buy 'em?" And the next thing I knew, I was doing trade shows from Seattle, Washington to Greenville, North Carolina. I guess someone had to help him sell all these clocks.

The real story begins with my friend, Harry, and I, heading out to our first trade show in Kamloops, British Columbia. It's a four-hour drive from my home near Lethbridge, Alberta, and after traveling several hours and discussing religious beliefs, we found ourselves at opposite ends of the spectrum on several issues. My friend was all for the big TV preachers that solicit for money, and he thought I should be listening to them too.

"I feel no need in my life to be filling my head with a lot of the stuff I've seen from these preachers," I told him. "A lot of these guys are con artists, milking the masses and using fear tactics to accomplish their wicked ends." (Now I don't condemn everyone on television. I have several personal favorites that have taught me a lot.)

"Sam, you need to get a TV and watch channel seventeen," Harry urged. "It has all kinds of excellent programs that you could learn from."

"I've got a Bible, Harry. God tells me that His Holy Spirit will guide me into all truth."

"Yeah, but they teach things about the Holy Spirit that you will never come up with yourself!" He insisted.

"Harry, I've seen God at work so often that my heart is overflowing. I already have all kinds of good books, I do a lot of memorizing and I'm not against learning. But with the way most of these TV evangelists are crashing and falling into gross sin, I just don't feel like having their ideas pumped into my home."

"Yeah, but there are some really good ones that you need to hear, especially the one that is talking about how the end of the world and the mark of the beast."

"Harry, can you imagine Jesus getting on national television and telling His congregation that He will die if He doesn't raise ten million dollars like the one preacher did?"

"Everybody makes mistakes, Sam. Don't you think that you need to freely forgive him? Why look at all the good he has done!"

"Forgive him or not, I want nothing to do with him. You can send him your money but don't expect me to! Just because someone does good it doesn't make them a good person. A lot of these people are frauds and false prophets and by their fruits, you shall know them, Harry."

"Don't be so judgmental, Sam. Give these people some room. Don't we all make mistakes?"

"Harry, did you see the fellow who prayed for gold teeth, and everyone in the congregation started yelling that they now have gold fillings? After the professor went to the dentist, they found out he was lying! He had the nerve to get behind the pulpit again and acted like nothing happened. These men are a reproach to everything I stand for and I don't want anything to do with them or support their lying ministries! Can't you get it?"

This conversation went up, down, and around the bend. Two people can have such a good time disagreeing.

We got to our destination, signed in to our motel, and Harry asked if he could watch his favorite channel. He had just turned it on when some guy started begging for money, claiming that his ministry was ready to close the doors if people didn't send money immediately. It's always the same story.

Did you know that God's work, done *God's* way, will never lack God's provision?

The TV con artist began to pray for funds and told the people to pray facing him because if they would pray towards the screen it would be like praying to God. I tried valiantly to convince Harry to pray towards the screen, but it was even too much for him!

The trade show was highly entertaining. There was a fortune teller we visited with. I've always wondered why they can't reveal the winning lottery numbers or just win it themselves? If they claim they can tell other people's futures, what about their own?

When the trade show was over, we packed up our booth and supplies and headed for the next town. We had been on the road for over an hour when I reached back over the seat and started groping for my briefcase.

"Harry," I said, "you'd better pull over. I can't find my briefcase! I think I left it on the running board of the truck. It's probably lying in the ditch between here and Penticton. Can I use your cell phone, please? I don't believe that God will let me lose everything in that case. That's not how He operates. This must have happened for a reason…maybe so you can see how good my Jesus is!"

It sure is strange what came to my mind as soon as I realized my briefcase was missing.

Not long before that, I had been walking down the street in windy Lethbridge, and there at my feet lay a wallet stuffed full of cash. There was only one problem: it also had a driver's license and personal identification. "Man, am I glad I never took a finder's fee," I said as I dialed the motel where we had stayed.

"Hello, this is Super 8. Would you care to make a reservation?"

"No thank you, but could you do me a favor? We stayed there the last three nights and when we were leaving, I forgot my briefcase on the running boards of our truck. Could you, would you, *please* see if it's lying on the street?"

Minutes passed in tense waiting as I wondered about the outcome. There were thousands of dollars plus all my future contacts and other important information in this briefcase. (Before cell phones, we had briefcases to keep everything together.) Wow, time flies. It seems like just yesterday briefcases were our "one-stop" solution.

"We're sorry Sir, but we walked all around our motel, and couldn't find your briefcase," the lady told me sympathetically.
I was about to hang up when she said, "Wait a minute! Someone is walking up the sidewalk carrying a black briefcase! Maybe it is yours!"

And it was! The lady that found it explained that she had been driving through a parking lot in the downtown area and saw this briefcase lying in the middle of the lot. She wanted to get a motel for the night and happened to come to the very motel where we had stayed, at the very same time I was on the cell phone, an hour and a half after we had left the motel! Absolutely amazing!

When I offered her to pay her, this dear soul told me she would never take one cent. She said someone had just returned her lost purse and would take nothing in return, so she would do the same. God bless you, dear lady!

Nothing is ever lost or secret when it comes to Jesus. The hard part is getting Him to show you where your lost items are.

Think about this, my friend. What are the odds that over an hour later, my briefcase would be found in a parking lot, because a lady came to the same motel where we had stayed at the same time I happened to call? Some would call this coincidence, but I don't think so!

If I would have taken money out of the wallet I found on the street, complete with the owner's identification, do you think this would have happened? I don't think so. The Golden Rule is still in effect; "Do unto others as you would have others do unto you." If you don't get your just dues here, you can still rejoice, because you will get them over there. I believe we often jump ship just before God comes through. When we get to Heaven, God will show us all the things we could have experienced if we would have just waited on Him and trusted in Him with all our heart.

My biggest problem is *waiting* on God or running ahead of Him. Often, when the going gets tough, I do things my way and forget about His. Then when God puts me in what I call the "God box" (when I have no place to turn to but God) I cry out to Him for help because my way has landed me in mega trouble.

It's like the time when I lost a whole ring of keys in a field of tall, thick alfalfa, which was almost ready to cut. There was no way humanly possible to locate them, so we whispered a prayer, walked about 100 feet into the field, reached down to part the alfalfa, and my hand fell right on the keys. When I told someone this story, they told me they had lost one of their contact lenses while swimming. They prayed and found a clear lens *in a pool!* God cares about lost keys, and lost contacts.

Sometimes the story doesn't end the way we want it to, and we never find out why God allows certain things. One year we had our summer camp-out a couple hours north of home and my daughter was the designated driver. She had to leave a day early to be at work on time, *but* she left with the only set of keys for that car! No amount of praying started the car or unlocked the steering wheel. Sometimes the answer is to use what God has placed between our ears.

Often we get frustrated and angry over misplacing something, or else we put it in such a good place that we forget where that "good place" was! Maybe we're too proud or unbelieving to pray but it seems like praying is a last resort. But then a few minutes after prayer, we find it.

When the man in the Bible lost a borrowed axe head, the prophet Elisha, threw a stick into the water and the axe head floated up to it (2 Kgs 6:1-7). Many people don't believe this can happen today because they don't know the living Jesus. He is just as alive and just as powerful today as He ever has been! If He takes care of us with such trifling little things as briefcases, key rings, and contact lenses, how much more is He willing to help us with bigger things? I am a slow learner, but I know this is true.

24¼ X 17½

This may be the strangest title you've ever seen, but maybe not. I wouldn't bet on it.

I'm reading a book on how to lower blood pressure naturally, written by a doctor from Texas. She states that you need to take time twice a day to sit down, stop your racing mind, and be so still that you can hear the breath coming in and out of your lungs as you inhale and exhale.[3] Try it once when your blood pressure is too high. Sit down and take thirty deep breaths into your lungs by compressing your stomach, not your chest, then slowly exhale and see what happens to your blood pressure.

It's amazing! I've brought mine down at least twenty percent in just one relaxing session. You wonder, why the blood pressure tip? Don't worry; there's no charge. I'm sharing what I've learned because it's so good for your health and well-being. Stop your world! Go throw some ribs or pork butt on the smoker and relax for a few hours alone. Use this time to communicate with your Maker!

I was smoking some ribs one clear, beautiful evening under the night sky. The stars twinkled like jewels scattered thickly over the inky blackness behind them, and the Milky Way was spectacular! It was so peaceful, so relaxing, and very serene just to watch the smoke as it billowed up into the heavens, to be able to have all my thoughts centered in a current moment of time.

When you gaze into the night sky, you realize that there are billions and *trillions* of stars and galaxies, millions and billions of

---

[3] (Merritt 2017)

light-years away. If you compare yourself, you feel very small and fragile and so insignificant! The Hubble telescope discovered stars so massive that Mt. Everest or Mt. McKinley would be less than a mere pinprick in one of these incomprehensible mega-monsters' valleys.

God's word tells us that the universe and all that is therein is the work of God's fingers, (Ps. 8:3) and He could create another universe just like this one by simply speaking the words. It would instantly be accomplished! Substances obey His commands! Things that have no minds, no will, and no emotions adhere to His slightest wishes. Someone, somewhere in my past, said, *"Only men and demons dare to disobey the Almighty."*

On this particular evening, it was nearing midnight; the ribs were almost done, and I was looking up, talking to my God. I said, "Lord, you are so big and strong and SO-O-O mighty, there's nothing that You can't do! I know there's an endless universe out there and a big world that You're looking after, but if You don't mind, dear God, I need a little touch! Just a token, or something that assures me that You and I are in touch and that You are hearing me!" I finished smoking the ribs and wrapped them up in tin foil. Then I cleaned everything up and tried to catch some sleep.

Now, I enjoy fixing up equipment in my spare time, restoring and reselling it, hopefully with a profit. I had purchased a 5050 *Allis Chalmers* tractor with a loader and a bush hog from a farmer about eighty miles away. The bush hog needed a lot of work because it was worn through here and there.

I began the restoration process by straightening out the bent metal around the outside edges, then putting on some new runners or skid plates on the bottom. The top of the bush hog needed to have some holes patched, so I decided to get a sheet of steel to cover the whole area that was worn through instead of patching a bunch of small holes.

The bottom of a bush hog has twin blades that are over two inches thick and so powerful that they can mulch saplings. This leaves the top of the mower the only place to put upright girders on it, so the unit has strength. I measured in-between the uprights and concluded that I needed a flat plate of steel, 24 ¼ inches by 17 ½ inches, to slide down between the uprights.

We live in a close-knit community where we all know each other and help each other out. My neighbor owns a body shop where they repair damaged vehicles, and I knew he had a few scraps of metal kicking around. So, I jumped on the four-wheeler and headed his way. I arrived at the neighbor's place and asked him if I could look around. "Help yourself, Sam," he said. "There might be something on the steel pile that you can use." I spied one piece of useable steel plate that looked like it might work. My good neighbor didn't charge me for it, so I loaded it up and headed home.

24 ¼ by 17 ½

Back at the shop, I looked at the opening on the bush hog where I needed to patch, then at the plate in my hand, and said to myself, *"This looks mighty close."* I set it inside the opening. It was a perfect fit! I called my wife, my business partner, and his son to come out to the welding shop, and we threw a measuring tape on that piece of steel. It measured a perfect 24 ¼ x 17 ½! My plea to God the night before came back to me. *"God! I need a little touch, a little token, or just something extra from You!"* There it was! The machine had come from eighty miles away and needed a piece of steel that just happened to be the only piece in my neighbor's yard, one that fit to the eighth of an inch! What's the probability of that? Thank you, thank you, Jesus! We're not alone down here!

Isn't it awesome that God dwells inside of us in the form of the sweet Holy Spirit if we believe in Jesus? Isn't it wonderful that Jesus lives in our hearts? He not only fills the heavens, but our bodies are His house, His temple, His Holy of Holies.

How then should we live our lives?

SPIRITUAL ILLUSIONS

Why are all the people smiling at me and acting so jovial?

While living next door to the majestic Rocky Mountains in windy southern Alberta, Canada, every season was well defined. Winter temperatures could drop below 40°, and you'd be dealing with stalled vehicles, frozen water troughs, jelling propane, and a host of other things that come with extreme cold. I remember when -40° F wouldn't stop us from shoveling off an out-door skating rink and then playing hockey till our feet were numb blocks of ice! Eventually, the local town became civilized and built a large indoor skating arena, which allowed hockey games to be a lot faster, warmer, and much more enjoyable.

Yes, *yes!* Hockey night in Canada was what winter was all about. Our generation experienced so-o-o many things that the kids nowadays won't know anything about. Ha! Besides hockey, hunting coyotes, and doing chores, winter in the Rockies has another amazing sport—snow skiing!

You can find a few decent ski slopes in the mid-western or eastern USA, but most of the time, you spend your days going down bunny hills. Out west, you'll soon discover what I mean when I say you can travel for miles and miles on one trip down the mountain. Often, on the ski slopes in Fernie, British Columbia, the mountain top would be shrouded in thick clouds with heavy snow falling. But down by the service plaza, it was pleasantly warm! Fernie has a yearly average snowfall of nine to thirty feet, and the top of the slope is seven thousand feet high.

I'll never forget the first time my buddies and I attempted to ski! Our first lift was to the very top of the mountain, up to where the only way down was the wicked slope they called *The Boomerang*. From the top, it looked like you'd almost free-fall as you pushed over that precipice. When you grow up playing hockey like I did, you can learn to ski easier because it's all about shifting your weight the right way. The learning curve had us going down from the very top all day. The fantastic wipeouts and spills throughout the day were epic, and pretty soon, we discovered we were hooked!

Now, I married a gorgeous young woman from Pennsylvania, and to date her, I had to drive 2,600 short miles. This was also considered extreme, but what's new? What do 2,600 miles matter? Don't let that stop you!

Well, my beautiful sister, who is just a year older than I, also met and married a fellow from the same area as my wife, and they ended up living in southern Alberta.

So, one fine winter weekend, I ask my brother-in-law if he'd like to try skiing in the Rockies. He never hesitated, but jumped at the chance. I must admit that he truly impressed me for not being a hockey player and coming from the far east. First, he went down the bunny hill a few times; then he tried the next level, and then went on to a more difficult run. Around noon I met up with him, and he told me he was so tired and wondered how long I planned to ski. I had planned to stay the whole day, so I decided to at least get a couple more runs in before calling it quits. At that point, I noticed that he was wearing a pair of brown polyester jeans that seemed to shed water real good. "How do you stay warm in them things?" I asked him. "Aren't you cold and wet?"

"Oh, I've got long johns on," he replied nonchalantly. Then he just took off and skied swiftly towards the lift.

As he skied away, I saw to my utter horror that his nice pair of polyester pants were split down the middle and that his long johns, which had to be two sizes too big, were billowing out the back. So now it was brown polyesters with big old white cotton sticking out between two buns. I knew if I'd hollered, he would've made a mad dash for the truck, so I casually suggested, "We'll go up as high as you dare and get a good run."

As we were riding the lift, he looked over at me and said, "People are so polite and friendly around here."

"What do you mean?" I wondered.

"Well, when they see me, they just break into the biggest smile and tell me to go ahead of them, so I usually do."

We rode to the top and skied down two more times. "One more run, brother-in-law," I urged. This time we were almost on top of the mountain, swinging our legs as the lift took us above some clouds.

My timid, self-conscious brother-in-law said, "Thanks, Sam. It's been an awesome day! I've never seen such friendly people in all my life. Even the girls smile at me." I could tell he was in his element, high as the mountain itself! "Do you think my spirit radiates such joy that people like to be around me?" he asked. "Do you think they can tell I'm a Christian, or what's going on?"

Knowing this was our last trip down the mountain, I waited till we were almost at the top when I asked, "My dear brother-in-law, when was the last time you checked your crotch? On the last three trips, everyone wanted you to go first as they smiled at you, but it's not because of any spiritual aura surrounding you or any mystical halo! Your brown, water-shedding, polyester pants have been split from top to bottom, and your waistband is basically all that's holding them up. The reason people are smiling from ear to ear is the free entertainment you're providing as you visit with them, introduce yourself, tell them what you do for work, where you live, that you originated from Pennsylvania, and that it's your first time skiing. They really believe you!"

He stared at me, shocked! "What should I do, what should I do?" he asked frantically as he went through his limited options. "I'm skiing down to the truck because I can't stay on the top of the mountain."

"I guess that's your only option," I agreed.

Normally, a skier goes from side to side as they gracefully ski down the steep slopes of the Rockies, so they don't pick up too much speed, but not that day! Not my dear brother-in-law! He pointed his skis straight ahead, leaned forward, and disappeared from sight in a moment. Me? Well, I prayed all the way down the mountain that he would somehow make it to the bottom without wrapping himself around a tree, or worse yet, another skier!

Sure enough, I got to the bottom, and there stood my brother-in-law, grinning like a possum, with his coat wrapped around his butt. "Let's get out of here," he said.

Be very careful. When strangers smile at you broadly and insist that you to go ahead of them on the ski slopes, make sure that you don't have your head in the clouds and forget normal living and how it goes! Haha! And have a mental checklist if everybody's giving you big smiles!

TOILET PAPER THIEF

My lovely bride was born and raised in the lush, beautiful, green hills near Hanover, Pennsylvania. She had a great life and a vibrant church group that reached out to the community. She had lots of friends, an incredible social life, a very good job, and a healthy, close-knit family where the parents loved each other and faithfully served the Lord.

Then suddenly, she was unceremoniously deposited smack-dab in the middle of a flat, 640 acre stubble field in a unsightly little house with no lawn or flowers or trees, and with no friends or family close by. It was just an endless, flat, dusty prairie where she could see her dog running away for two days—if she had a dog. It must have been a total shock to leave all that beauty and security, a great social life with friends and family, to move across America to windy, harsh southern Alberta.

Our house (that Jack built) was on a bit of a hill, and we could see the Rocky Mountains to the west, the Milk River Ridge to the south, and flat prairies to the north and east. Folks often wonder how far you can see on a clear day. Standing on my doorstep, you could see the top of Crow's Nest Mountain, and it's at least a eighty miles away.

I really miss the weather patterns of the prairies since we have moved away. You could look to the northwest and watch a storm forming from start to finish. Here in the south, a storm sweeps up over the hill and arrives so fast you hardly see it coming. About once a year, we would make the long trek from Raymond, Alberta through Montana, into northern Wyoming, across South Dakota,

Minnesota, Illinois, Indiana, Ohio, and finally into south central Pennsylvania to visit my wife's family.

My grandmother's branch of the Glanzer family came from the area around Mitchell, South Dakota, where many of the business owners and bankers share the same surname. We have some very good Hutterite friends who run a large turkey farm just south of there. Their farm was approximately halfway to our destination, so we'd end up staying overnight at the colony. We'd always have a wonderful visit, lots of good food, and a warm feather bed in which to rest our travel-weary bones.

On one particular journey across the states, we arrived at the colony, spent one night, and prepared to leave in the morning. "What's the rush?" everyone was asking. "The fun is just beginning. You can play guitar for us again tonight! Life is short; stay a few more days!" So, they convinced us to stay for several more days so we could get to know them better. The colony doesn't allow musical instruments, but the young people started begging the minister early in the afternoon to let us sing a song or two. Finally, around eight o'clock in the evening, he agreed to let us play a couple of tunes. I figured this wasn't a very good paying proposition, begging for five hours and only getting in two songs, but in the end, we played a whole lot more than two!

It turned into a whole evening of singing, and at midnight the preacher said to me, as he was holding his good wife's hand, "Sam, we're in trouble anyway, so could you play another love song before we go to bed?" No one enjoys music more than those who are not allowed to have it.

The next morning, we were invited to the big kitchen, where everyone would gather to eat the three meals of the day. Right beside me sat an old English fellow, sucking on a chicken bone as though it were the last bone on Earth and he was living in a Russian prison camp. He kept making these awful mouth noises, his teeth clattered, and the spit was bouncing everywhere as he tried to suck the marrow right out of the bones, leaving nothing nutritious for the colony dogs to scavenge.

Now, I've got a weak stomach to begin with, and sitting next to him, my appetite vanished. No one else seemed to mind; they all seemed to be used to him. I used to slop the pigs when I was a kid, and sitting beside this dude took me right back to my childhood as I poured the warm, fresh milk into the hog's trough. The squealing and grunting and slobbering were nearly identical to this fellow's inelegant way of eating.

In a colony, you usually eat the main meal in the community kitchen, then go back to the private homes with your friends for a coffee or a little dessert. When we got back to the house, my friend said, "Sam, I see you didn't eat much dinner today. Did that guy bother you by the way he was carrying on?" I was kind of embarrassed, but I told my friend that I had indeed lost my appetite. He laughed and said, "Do you have a clue who this fellow is?"

"Not a clue."

"He's one of the largest land-owners and richest men in South Dakota! The banks wish they had his money."

"Interesting!" I said.

"Let me tell you about a trip my brother and I took with this fellow up to Rochester, Minnesota," he continued. "We were staying at a motel together. He got up and showered before my brother and I could get out of bed. The first thing I saw as I opened my eyes was this man's big hairy ass as he was bending over his suitcase, stark naked, trying to cram all the motel's towels, toilet paper rolls, shampoo, and soap into his suitcase! I got up and went into the washroom, and every single thing in the bathroom was gone except the shower curtain. I said, 'Harold! I've got to have a towel and toilet paper and soap!' He tore off a few squares of paper and handed them to me, broke a bar of soap in half, and fished out a small face cloth."

"Then what?" I asked, trying not to let my naturally inquisitive mind get too visual.

"I said, 'Harold, this just won't do! It wouldn't even wipe a baby's butt, let alone a grown man's! And my brother needs to freshen up too.' He just stood there for a while and stared, trying to settle in his mind what he could spare. Then he threw me a roll of toilet paper and a towel and said, 'That's all you guys are getting!' so we had to make do."

My mother used to tell a story about a man that they knew who was on his death bed. Suddenly, he sat up in his bed and said, *"Brother John got more than I did!"* Then, he sank back and died.
I worked with two brothers who were working out a business deal, and the person on the other end of said deal was their very own father. "Your father is going to lose a lot of money if this deal goes through," I told them. "Oh, he has enough," they said.

The love of money is definitely something that will lower a man into such a depraved state that his own family, friends, and neighbors are not safe around him. He will bulldoze over everyone in his path to gain what he cannot keep. Money becomes his god.

But back to my story!

"Would you like to go meet this old fellow?" my friend asked.

"Sure, why not?" I said. That evening after dark, we went for a drive in the country, down this long dirt trail with tall weeds bordering both sides. A mile down this neglected old trail, we came to this shack, literally hidden amongst the weeds.

"This is where he lives," my friend said. My friends knocked on the door, gave their names, and were told to come in.

As they opened the door, they said, "Harold, we have a friend with us."

Harold was lying on his bed with a shotgun pointed right at my stomach. My friends yelled, "He's ok, he's ok!" Harold pointed the gun away. After a short visit, and we headed back to the colony.

"Why would such a wealthy man live in an old pig sty?" I wondered aloud.

"He's terrified that someone's going to get some of his money," they explained.

"But he's old and decrepit, and he'll soon leave it all," I said.

If I live to be 500, I will never forget that night. That old, lonely man, holed up in a dirty shack somewhere on the prairies of South Dakota, hanging onto his money with the last bit of strength he could muster! How pitifully sad. Later on, this poor rich Harold lent two of his neighbors some money, but they didn't pay him back, so he shot them both, went to prison, and died there. What a miserable ending for a miserable soul!

The book of Colossians, chapter three, tells us to set our affection on things above, not on things of this Earth (Col. 3:2). He was definitely one of those poor, rich men that we see everywhere!

SON OF A SEACOOK

GETTING RID OF THE GREEN

My "fabulous forties" were busy years. I'd be home for a week or two, and then I'd be in different areas holding meetings or street preaching in distant cities.

Now, I'm a finicky man with a very weak stomach. My good wife and I have our living quarters pristine most of the time, and taking a shower once a day is a priority for me. When I'm eating, I prefer pleasant, agreeable conversation because of my vivid imagination. My dad didn't allow us to mention dogs or cats at the table; it just grossed him out!

We have hosted many strangers through the years and have had to teach some of them the value of shampooing, showering, watching your words, and minding your manners at the dinner table. One young fellow in particular would plunge his knife into the honey or the jam jar, lick it off, and go in for seconds. That is not allowed at my table! Ha! Another young guest was eating red beets and expounding about the first time he ate them and how he thought he was bleeding inside when he used the washroom. *Yikes!* Again, not acceptable at my table, or I'll leave. When we're together as a family, and people want to get a laugh at my expense, they'll talk about things that are right on the edge of being tolerated. What's so funny about that?

I've improved with age, but still have times when my stomach involuntarily shuts down and my hunger evaporates. If a person pulls two or three long hairs out of a dinner bun or the food looks like slop, it's easy for me to skip a meal. And I fully realize that children in North Korea dig through cow poop just to find some undigested corn! This should never happen in our world, but starving people will shove about anything in their mouths just to stop the horrible hunger. I've read about people who were imprisoned for long periods of time and left to starve to death. They tell how God kept them alive by bringing big rats into their cell, which they ate raw without becoming sick!

Lord Jesus! We take time right now just to thank You and praise You for how good You've been to us! Please forgive us for grumbling or complaining in any way! Thank you, Jesus!

I was traveling with some friends through an eastern state in the USA, and someone suggested we stop at a mutual friend's house for supper if it suited them. We all agreed. To this day, I'm still in shock at the stench and the filth of that place! They had a week's worth of dried-on dishes piled in the sink, the countertops were overflowing with junk, and the floor was so greasy you had to walk carefully to keep your balance! Please don't make me describe the washroom conditions! My poor stomach gave a sickening lurch, and even though they ordered in pizza, I couldn't eat a bite. I had never in all my life experienced something so disturbing and disgusting! But wait! It gets more interesting!

Several times back in the nineties, we took a large group of young folks to Los Angeles, California, to spend a week feeding the homeless, working at the big missions, washing, cleaning, and handing out gospel tracts. Every evening we'd get together, and Mr. Ray Comfort would arrive and give us pep talks, a lot of laughs, and loads of inspiration.

One evening Ray asked, "Hey, do you guys want to be super-spiritual?"

"Yes!" we all agreed. "We're all in!"

"There's a place in Inglewood where the parents both died of cancer, and the invalid daughter, who also has cancer, is living there alone. You need to go see if you can help."

The next morning, everyone in the group headed for downtown LA to a new and unforgettable experience. We got to the house, all eager to start, and immediately the police showed up and inquired what we were doing in that part of town. "We always come here by two and threes," they told us. "You need to be extra careful because this is a high crime area. There's a lot of fighting between the local gangs."

The house looked like any other house on the street, so some of us went in to assess the situation. We opened the door, and the stench that hit us was worse than anything I'd ever smelled. Garbage was stacked from floor to ceiling. There was no telling if the floor was dirt, linoleum, or tile because scum completely covered it. The path through the house was so narrow we had to walk single file. Cats were running everywhere, sitting on the window sills and slinking behind the doors. Things were moving and making strange noises under the trash, and I was expecting a boa constrictor to crawl out at any moment.

We immediately hired a one-ton truck to haul out the garbage, bought a ton of face masks, and went to work. We unearthed cats that had died years ago, cats that had recently died and were half rotten, and one decomposing cat whose bowels were showing through its skin! My friend scooped it up with a big corn shovel only to find that the poor thing was still alive! I shudder at the memory.

Then we shoveled out the fridge. There was rotting hamburger meat, moldy jars of mayonnaise, ketchup, and green bread. You name it; it was all there. It was festering, rotting, stinking, and full of disease. We had to shovel the floor before we could even begin to use a broom or wash it. God bless the dear girls who cleaned that floor! We hauled tons of garbage, cat feces, dead rotting cats, and hideous trash and hauled it to a dump somewhere in that big city. This became the *Number One*, most despicable situation I had ever encountered. At the close of the day, we had to ride home in the back of the pick-up trucks because no one could sit in the tight quarters of a cab and keep breathing. The stench was just too rancid.

Number Two on my most disgusting list goes like this. I was in a certain place without plumbing, but they did have five-gallon pails with pot lids covering them. Beside the bucket you used was a pail of wood shavings, and when you were finished, you were expected to put shavings on top of your mess. Well, I hated the situation, but there was no other option. So, when I was done using the bucket, I saw two pails of shavings beside me. I reached in to grab some shavings and sank my hand in a pail of poop that hadn't been emptied yet. Now, there was no running water in the cabin where I slept, and here I had put my hand deep down in the wrong pail! I desperately needed somewhere to clean up! Somehow, I managed to pull up my pants and button them with my left hand, trying all the while not to touch anything with my right hand till I found some way to sanitize it.

I promise you; I never chewed my fingernails for many moons after that episode. I wasn't able to tell this story for years because it was just too gross, but I recently told it for the first time to some of my nieces and nephews in Philadelphia. They shrieked and screamed with laughter. That same evening, as we were getting ready to leave, we hugged, shook hands, and I squeezed my niece's cheek. She let out a scream and said, "You touched me with the same hand that you reached into that pail with!"

"Yes," I said, "but that was over twenty years ago."

Now for my *Number Three* most despicable, disgusting, and unforgettable experience. I once held meetings in an Amish community where several families had left their horse and buggy roots for a more modern lifestyle. Now they could have things like electricity, refrigerators, cars and all the fancy doodads that we take for granted.

After the morning service, we gathered for a potluck dinner. Some dishes looked safe and delightful, but others looked like they had a week of someone's left-overs dumped into one pot. I had just taken a generous plateful of food that looked good and safe when one fine gentleman approached and asked if I had tried his wife's turkey gravy. I asked what dish it was, and he told me, so I poured it all over my food and sat down to eat. I was almost done eating and thinking about a little dessert when the same fellow came up to me and asked, "How was the gravy? My wife sure is a good cook, isn't she?"

"She sure is," I agreed. "That gravy was excellent!"

The man sat down across from me, and we visited about this and that. "Sam, did I ever tell you what happened to us last week?" he asked.

"No...tell me."

"Well, we butchered our turkeys and filled up our big deep freezer before we went back east to see my folks. When we got home, we realized the power had been out the whole time. All those turkeys were covered with green slime, but we cut it all off and saved what we could. Oh, it was a mess! You didn't taste anything funny, did you, Sam?" I almost threw up in his lap. I could feel all that gravy trying to shoot up the elevator, and I tried fiercely to keep it down. I excused myself, jumped in my vehicle, and flew down the road, looking for a place to stop. I think it's called projectile vomiting.

Now, years later, every time I go out to eat, his solemn words keep ringing in my ears, *"We cut off all the green."* At least it helps me keep a trim waistline. And I have to remember that all men are created differently. We all have different natures, different levels of tolerance, and vastly different upbringings. God makes no mistakes. Every living soul was planned and formed and fashioned by His Almighty hand! All things do work out for the good of those who love the Lord.

A TWENTY-FIVE YEAR OLD GUILTY CONSCIENCE

Here is a thrilling little story my dad told me at least six times. Years later, he would say, "I still can't believe how fast it happened. I asked God, and the very next day, I met the man!"

Things were definitely done differently when my father was a young man. He said their neighbor's livestock was always running loose on their property. No matter how often they asked the neighbor to fix his fences, his animals kept showing up. Well, one fine day, this neighbor's gaunt, crippled, skinny horse showed up behind the barn where Grandfather kept his pigs. Dad, who happened to be feeding the pigs, caught the old nag, put a blindfold on it, and killed it with one mighty blow of a sledgehammer. The hogs had a feast of fresh horse meat that afternoon!

No sooner had Dad finished the grisly deed and stepped through the front door of the barn when the neighbor man drove up, looking for his old mare. "Hey, Sammy! You haven't seen my old black mare around here anywhere, have you?"

"Nope, haven't seen a thing," he lied.

"She strayed off again, and I need to find her."

Dad stood at the door and watched him drive slowly out of sight, a little shook up by what had just happened. For the next twenty-five years, God faithfully reminded him of the lie he had told. Finally, he could stand it no longer. He got down on his knees and asked God to help him find this fellow so that he could confess the wrong and clear his conscience. "Lord, if you let me see the neighbor man, I'll talk to him," he prayed.

That day, he drove into town, went into the general Farm Supply store, and guess who opened the door for him? The neighbor man, who he had not seen for twenty-five years!

Lord! Not quite this soon!

Dad took the neighbor man aside and told him he had killed his horse, and my dad asked him if he could pay for it. He told Dad that he knew all along that he had killed his horse and that he was forgiven. The man said, "Sammy, give me fifty bucks, and we'll call it square."

Dad paid him for the horse, shook his hand, and thanked him. Dad told me, "I felt like I was walking on air! The sun was shining brighter, the birds were chirping louder, and my heart was singing!" Just a week later, the neighbor's obituary appeared in the *Lethbridge Herald*.

God does care. God will move. God wants to help us, but do we want His help?

Another acquaintance was hospitalized for the tenth time, trying to figure out why he was always so sick. The doctors did every test on him they could think of, but he kept declining. One day, he confessed to his wife that he had cheated on her, and all his adverse symptoms disappeared! He lived to a ripe old age.

I stole a few items when I was a kid, and my mind tormented me until I made it right. Oh, the peace and joy of a clean conscience! Recently I was driving with our five-year-old granddaughters and telling them about Pinocchio and how his nose grew whenever he told a lie. Without missing a beat, the one twin said, "Grandpa, I lie, and my nose don't grow!"

Of course, I explained that Pinocchio was just a fairytale, and she said, "A fairytale is just like a lie, Grandpa. Isn't it?"

"Yup…it is." I agreed. "How do you feel when you tell a lie?" I asked her.

"I feel so terrible until I tell Mother," she said. Out of the mouth of babes comes more truth than from a lot of adults!

Which sinful pleasure, which stolen item, which lie is worth the unbearable price of a guilty conscience? We need to realize that life is but a vapor, and we need to make the best of the time we have. We need to make sure our conscience is clear! We should be hard on ourselves and easy on others.

Love ya all!

SON OF A SEACOOK

NEVER SAY "WHOA" IN A MUDHOLE

My father was born in 1923 in Lethbridge, Alberta, Canada. I recall that he left home at the tender age of fifteen with his younger brother, George.

Dad told me that he worked for a while at a nearby German prison camp, hauling away the garbage with a horse and a cart. He had to pass a security guard at the exit gate every time he left with a load, and this guard would vigorously stab around the garbage with a big, sword-like knife to make sure no prisoners were hiding under the trash. (Ouchy, Ouchy…that would hurt!)

About fifteen years later, Dad was married and settled on a farm about half an hour from where he grew up. When the stork brought all of us kids into the scene, my parents' lives got really full and interesting!

I had to think of our youngest daughter, who was living foot-loose and fancy-free when she started dating this fine gentleman. He was also living on a roll, working the oil rigs in the north and making big bucks which he spent as fast as he made them. You would think he didn't have a care in the world.

When our daughter and this boyfriend wanted to go skiing for the weekend, they went! Or if they felt like going to a hockey game or a concert it was no big deal; they did that too. Yup, just dream it up and do it! I said to them, " Man you guys live like high rollers."

Be still and listen, as those days quickly came to an end. They got married and a couple of years later on a Sunday afternoon, this same daughter of ours said, "Dad, ah…you're going to be a Grandpa again."

"Whoa! Wonderful, wonderful!" I told her.

"Dad, you don't get it!" she said with her big blue eyes shining. "You're going to be a *double* Grandpa! We're expecting twins! How will we ever take care of two at once?"

In due time, two beautiful baby girls arrived! And a year later, on a Sunday afternoon I heard, "Daddy, you're going to be a Grandpa again!" And those blue eyes were *really* shining.

"Really? Wonderful, wonderful!" I told her.

"No Daddy, you don't quite understand!"

"Oh no!" I thought. "What now?"

"It's twins again!"

Two years and four precious children. *Boom, boom, BOOM!*

No more jet-setting lifestyle, no more big concerts and hockey games and weekend skiing trips! Now they both work, eat, change diapers, walk the floor all night, wake up groggy, change more diapers, endure the constant crying, screaming, fighting….you get the picture.

It's like, *"Dad, can you and Mom take the kids for a while? We need a break or we'll go nuts!"*

You get the picture—a little bit of innocent lovin' and what a pickle you can get yourself into! Boom, crash, boom, with no one to blame but themselves! Haha...love it!

What would they possibly do without Grandpa and Grandma? Or like the grand kiddies call us, *"Booboo"* and *"Pada."*

Just like my parents; stuck...or blessed rather...with five little kids. Not only did they have to meet each other's needs, but the wants and needs of five little people.

Of course, once we got older and realized our own existence, we also became aware of our surroundings. Our home place had a nice irrigation canal running through the middle of it, all kinds of farm animals, and about 3,400 acres to explore on horseback. Talk about a young child's paradise! The canal became a large part of our childhood and in my young mind, it was the best thing a kid could ever have. We floated homemade wooden rafts, spent hours swimming with all our friends, and even caught a sucker or two.

My dad said that during the war, there used to be a huge German prison camp not far upstream, and the same canal that flowed through our farm also ran through the camp. (I guess we could call it the underwater railroad for German prisoners.)

Dad said sometimes a bucket would come floating along, and under the bucket was a prisoner of war with just his head above water. These prisoners would sneak out, work all day for a farmer, then head back into the prison camp for the night. The guards would just look the other way.

Many years later, I had the privilege of meeting some of these German prisoners who stayed in Canada, got their families to join them, and became very successful businessmen.

One of our German friends who stayed was a gentleman by the name of William, who started an extremely successful diesel shop in our home town.

Dad was also an excellent mechanic, and he would often stop in to visit with William and learn from him as he'd tear engines apart and put them back together again.

William was a *Messerschmitt* pilot during the war. He was shot down, but survived the parachute landing and was captured, and shipped to a prison camp in faraway western Canada, where he lived happily until his death.

Dad said some of these prisoners, were so-o-o brilliant that they could build radios out of tin cans and other pieces of discarded garbage. That way they could keep abreast of the war news.

Ironically, the Germans treated their prisoners of war in the most horrible, gruesome fashion, but here in Canada, the German prisoners were treated better than they ever had been in their motherland.

Another story Dad enjoyed telling was about his uncle who owned two greyhound dogs. One day Dad was carrying a five-gallon pail as he was walking towards the big white barn. Uncle's greyhounds were madly chasing a rabbit around and around the barn, closing the gap with each round. Dad quickly put the pail between his knees and faced the direction of the poor, terrified, on-coming rabbit. That unfortunate rabbit was completely out of options, thought that the pail was a hole, and hit it at breakneck speed, (pun intended) then dropped over, deader than a doornail.

Dad related how his father was plowing one stormy day with his team of horses. For some reason, the horses stopped right in the middle of plowing, turned their heads, and looked back at him. At that very moment, a bolt of lightning went through the one horse's head, killing him instantly. If those horses hadn't turned their heads, the lightning would have killed his father!

Talk about lightning strikes! I was fishing from a boat in the middle of a lake back in the mountains when a group of trail riders on horseback rode past. The caravan of horses was just entering the woods on the southern edge of the lake, when a tremendous bolt of lightning shot up from the ground, through the horse and his rider, instantly killing them both!

I learned that day that lightning can also come up from the ground to meet the charge from the sky above. The poor fellow probably never knew what hit him. Talk about a sudden change of life. One moment you're riding a horse in the breathtakingly beautiful Rocky Mountains, talking and visiting with your friends, and a split second later you're in eternity, facing your Creator! It's actually a good, painless way to go *IF* you're ready to meet God.

Now a little from the lighter side of life. I remember how helplessly Dad would laugh when he started reminiscing. Laughing so hard made him really cough and he would have to lean forward to catch his breath. This happened often when some of his old cronies would show up, and they would start to tell their stories.

Let's get back to my intended story!

Things were always happening on the farm where we grew up, and this particular day was a very special one. Our house had been sitting on a foundation with just a crawl space, and Dad had built a basement about a quarter-mile away, where he planned to add a kitchen to the house once it was moved. The basement plus the kitchen would provide ample room for our growing family.

Before the house was moved, we could look out our living room window and easily see right into our beloved neighbor's kitchen. Two rows of houses faced each other with a sidewalk (perfect for bike rides) in between. At the east end of the sidewalk, was the community church, and on the west end of was Grandma's house, where there was always a glass of cold water, ice-cream treats, or a Band-Aid, if you needed one.

I was so excited, I couldn't eat my cornflakes quick enough, so in my hurry to get outside and watch all the action, I ended up drinking them, and almost choked.

The first things to greet my eager young eyes and ears were all the big winch trucks and tractors, and the men who were yelling at each other, as they proceeded to raise the house off of the foundation, and set it on the large moving beams. There was so much noise you'd have thought we were moving the Egyptian pyramids!

Excerpt: ***Men yell because they need to feel important and because they like the sound of their own voice. It fills them with confidence and stirs an adrenaline rush. Does not even nature teach you? Just listen to the king of the beasts, and what do you hear? A MIGHTY ROAR! It's the same with every male; it comes from the depths of his male instinct to conquer, to experience great adventure, and to live on the edge the way God intended him to.***

I knew a fellow way back when, who kind of overdid it. He was an extremist who wrecked things for the honest yellers, or fellers. The guy got goosebumps all over his body and you'd think he was going to hyperventilate from the thrill of hearing his own musical voice.

Many times you'd think you heard the conversation, and that there was a crowd nearby that had snuck up on you, but after checking to see what all the noise was about, or what party was in progress, you would come upon this dear fellow having the jolliest of times, happily talking to himself.

He was good to have around and work with because he could fix about anything, but he had a tremendous need to be someone special and not just another one of the several billion who inhabit this planet.

For many years, we all worked together with this dear soul, everyone doing the jobs delegated to them. But when strangers or businessmen would appear, he would randomly start shouting orders at the rest of us, as though we were all of a sudden stupid, and as if he ran the whole farm. The way he was ordering us around, with small details, it would have seemed like we all forgot how to tie our own shoes! When the people would leave, he'd sort of simmer down to his usual, barely audible mumblings, no doubt pacified by the momentary rush of fresh blood to his brain.

Why do we as humans try to act like we're so much better and way more important than the next man?

Right across the path where the house needed to go was the aforementioned canal. The water wasn't running yet, so the men filled a wide portion of the canal with dirt and packed it down real good to make a road so they could pull the house across.

The large beast of a machine that was pulling the house was a steel track tractor called the Emco. This enormous machine started pulling the house towards the canal, then hit a wet spot of ground, and instantly sank down in the mud till it was sitting on its frame…seriously high centered!

This was very exciting for a seven-year-old boy. I had the same attitude that my dad had as he was watching a spray plane one afternoon. He had just finished saying to himself, "I'd hate to see that thing crash, but if it's going to crash anyway, I'd like to see it happen." The words had barely left his mouth when that spray plane dumped all its chemicals and crash-landed in the field where he was standing.

Dad said the pilot successfully landed the plane, but as soon as he opened the hatch he started cursing violently. He climbed out of the wreck without a scratch! You'd think a man would fall on his face, kiss the ground, and thank God he was alive, but no...that would be sanely using your mind.

Cursing: *A weak mind trying to express itself.*

Again...my story!

The men tried for hours to pull this monster machine out of the soft muck but to no avail. They hooked up their winch trucks and the biggest four-wheel-drive tractors in the community, but it didn't budge one inch! It settled deeper, tighter, faster, and firmer than a blind, judgmental, critical professor stuck in the bog of his own self-righteousness.

A few men were still yelling at each other, trying to look important, but other than the meaningless shouting everyone got kind of quiet.

My dad, who had been watching all the efforts, walked up to the owner of the moving crew and said, "Mr. Kerner! What'll ya give me if I drive that machine out on its own power?"

"You've gotta be crazy Sam! What ya' been smokin'?"

Joe Kerner replied. "This machine is gonna need the army's biggest helicopter to lift it out!"

I guess they all agreed with Joe because my Dad got lots of laughs and some awfully funny looks.

"I'll give you a forty-ounce bottle of whiskey, Sam, if you can move that thing one inch," Joe grinned.

Dad looked at me with a little smile and said, "Watch this, Son!"

Things kicked into high gear as he took over the situation, and my chest swelled with pride as I watched a real man work instead of just make noise like so many of the wannabes.

"I need two of your strongest chains," Dad requested. "Two of you husky fellows lay that telephone pole in front of the Emco's tracks."

Never Say "Whoa" in a Mudhole - Young Sam with the house moving crew

Then Dad tied a chain to each track and securely around the pole, jumped up on the Emco, put it in first gear, and with one puff of black smoke, that monster machine pulled the telephone pole right under itself, and sat there, free of the mud hole.

Yes! Just like that! The crowd of wannabe's just stood there with their mouths kind of hanging open, not saying a word, just watching in a daze as my dad, grinning like a possum, drove this big machine all over the yard.

Often in my life I've seen hopeless situations where tragedy seemed imminent, and along came someone, gave a simple suggestion that no one else had thought about, and poof, the problem was solved.

It's like the semi-truck that was stuck underneath a bridge, and the grownups were trying unsuccessfully to pull it out. A little fellow nearby suggested that they let some air out of the tires, and after they did what he said, the truck rolled free on its own power.

Look at all the amazing inventions of our time—new technology, satellites orbiting the globe, the internet, cell phones, and countless other mind-staggering inventions. They all exist because someone was persistent, and never said *"whoa"* when he hit the mud holes, the setbacks, the disappointments, the failures, or whatever gets us discouraged.

Thomas Edison made a thousand light bulbs before one actually lit up, and that one was carried upstairs by a young lad who dropped and broke it. What did Thomas do? He grabbed the bull by the horns, painstakingly made another one, and gave the same boy another chance to transport the precious light bulb! Today, we all take light bulbs for granted, but trust me, the young feller never dropped it again.

What about the poor soul that you've been helping for years and they don't seem to improve or even want to better themselves? They're stuck in the mud hole of continuous bad decisions. Don't quit and don't give up, because where there's life, there's hope.

I recall a certain neighbor of ours that was as ungodly as a man could be. Everyone wrote him off and avoided him like the plague. One day we heard that the poor fellow died, and everyone was wringing their hands and thinking about how terrible it must be for him in the next life. My uncle and I had been working at the chicken barns and we were walking towards the mess kitchen when we saw this same man walking towards us.

What on earth? It's our ungodly neighbor who we thought was dead! We got closer and our neighbor began talking. "I'm here to tell you guys something!"

"But we heard you were dead!" My uncle blurted out.

"I was," he said earnestly. "When I woke up I found myself in the morgue cold room with a bunch of other dead people. You might not believe this but bedside each one of us was a *devil*...or a dark spirit, waiting to take us somewhere! I could see them! One was next to me! I was full of terror, in a body bag and cold as ice. I cried out to God to have mercy on me, and the next thing I know I'm being wheeled out of the morgue. They heard me hollering and discovered I was still alive and let me out! The main reason I'm here is to tell you about all the stuff I've stolen off this farm, and I'd like to make it right and return what I can."

If I remember right, he had stolen things we hadn't even missed.

"Can you forgive me?" he asked. "I've found Jesus and have peace with God, and now I'm ready to die."

He passed away soon after.

So my dear friend, never give up, and definitely never say *"WHOA"* in a mud hole!

Every mud hole you make it through will make you a better person and able to handle the next one with a lot more confidence.

WHEN GIVING DOESN'T MAKE SENSE

I'll admit that I was pretty wild and crazy in my younger days, and those who knew me best can relate. Music was my greatest addiction, or should I say my passion. I ate, slept, and awoke to the dream of becoming a musician. I don't know why it affected me and resonated so deeply with me, but it did!

One frigid winter, I broke my arm right in the middle of the hockey season, and since I couldn't play hockey, I decided to take a solo trip and explore the eastern seaboard of the big old USA. My older sister knew a certain girl in one of the distant eastern states and convinced me that she was super cute, very lovely, and definitely worth meeting. Here was one more good reason to drive the thousands of miles from southern Alberta, Canada, to the eastern USA. What could it hurt?

I don't know what clothes I packed or what else I took along for the long trip, but I do know I went around to several of my buddies, borrowing their eight-track tapes until I had a box full on the seat and another one on the floor. I wanted to have non-stop music all the way because that's what was important to me! You may say, "Forget about all the music! What about the girl? We're interested in the girl!"

Ok, ok! She was a beautiful, God-fearing, God-honoring young woman, and she wondered right away if I had a personal relationship with Jesus. That was her main focus and her primary concern. Mine was just a pretty face and a good time. I lost interest in her pretty quickly because I thought she was just another religious individual. Sorry to say, but I had already experienced many broken friendships, church splits, and religious fights from a very tender age, and my mind was closed to those who professed to be religious.

My rock music had become a safe place for me to hide. When it was pounding in my head, my world was okay, but every time the music stopped, the silence was deafening. I knew in my heart that I was not at peace, but kept pushing the God thoughts out of my mind as best I could. Oh, I always believed there was a God; I never doubted it. I just didn't like the folks who represented Him. If He was like them, then I figured He wouldn't like me either.

I tried my darndest to find satisfaction in many different ways aside from God, but I soon realized that no matter what I did, no matter what I tried, I'd always come up short, with this gnawing emptiness inside. Questions haunted me. *Is this all there is to life? Am I destined to go through life with things always going as they currently were?*

So, I became kind of a drifter, living in Missouri for a while, where some folks took me into their home and loved on me in a life-changing way, then Virginia and Pennsylvania, just doing odd jobs to survive. Something funny happened every place I went; I couldn't run away from it. I met real Jesus-loving people who I knew really cared about me. They were beautiful folks in every way. Each one told me that I needed Jesus and that I needed to know Him personally. Instead of *'you shouldn't do this,'* and *'you shouldn't do that,'* and *'we believe this,'* and *'we believe that,'* their message was clear.

"Sam?"

"Yes?"

"You need Jesus."

I asked them why are there 4,200 different denominations, and they all claim to have the one and only Jesus, and they can't get along with each other?? (Check out Ephesians 4, the first part of the chapter!)

Well, in my own heart, I knew that I didn't care if there were ten million denominations, I just knew I wasn't happy, and my fun wasn't cutting it anymore. Maybe my natural supply of endorphins was running low, and my adrenals glands were over-stressed. I don't know! I'm sure they were.

Writing that last line reminded me of what an old hippie said to me one day, "Sam, I wish you wouldn't have told us about Jesus, because since you did, I can't enjoy any of my parties anymore, and every time I sleep with a woman, I feel like the devil's in the room. Nothing turns me on anymore." That hippie had a sad, burned-out life. The poor soul went to eternity at the young age of fifty. I talked with him the day before he died and presented Jesus to him for about the fiftieth time, in the best way I could. All he said was, "Sam, I'm so-o scared, I'm so-o scared, why does it all have to end this way?"

Now, back to my story.

One day I made a choice. I took personal responsibility for my situation and decided to buy a little pocket Bible to find out for myself what it taught. I started reading with a vengeance. One day I read a verse in 1 John 1, and I know exactly where I was when I read it. I was on Interstate 81, driving from Harrisburg, Virginia, to Chambersburg, Pennsylvania.

*"And these things write we unto you, **that your joy may be full.***" *(1 Jn. 1:4 KJV)*

It rocked my world to the core. My mind and heart and my whole being cried out for that fullness of joy! I was ready to give in and hopefully bring my emptiness to an end. I said, "Lord Jesus, if You will give me this fullness of joy that this verse talks about, I will serve you forever." I felt an instant peace settle over my soul. Was I converted then and there? I don't know.

The next verse I found and camped on was in Isaiah 1:18. *"Come now, and let us reason together, saith the* **Lord:** *though your sins be as scarlet, they shall be as white as snow: though they be red like crimson, they shall be as wool."* I remember meditating on this verse so long that I knew it from memory. I would then tell God all my sins, how sorry I was that I did them, and ask for His forgiveness.

I felt a whole lot better and kept on faithfully reading until one day I read a passage from John 8:34, 35, and 36 where it says that *a servant can't abide in the house forever, but the son can.* I realized at that point that I was addicted to nicotine. One of the biggest battles in my life was getting rid of cigarettes. Eventually, I replaced the deadly pack of cigarettes with a small blue Bible, with a cover picture of Jesus holding little children on His lap. I literally gave up death for life.

Now, when my old partners in crime would want to bum a cigarette, I'd tell them I quit. "Well then, what's in your pocket?" they'd ask. I'd show them my little blue Bible and explain what had happened to me and what peace I had found through reading it.

Lo and behold, they asked me to get them one! I soon ordered small pocket Bibles by the case, twenty or fifty at a time, and passed them out. It didn't take long, and soon every time we'd get together, we'd talk about things we were finding in our Bibles. It became a common theme that we all loved the Jesus man, and none of us could stand the Scribes and Pharisees. Or should I say the religious professors?

The wheels of time kept turning, and I was back home in Canada, driving past a certain business establishment, and a little voice in my head said, "Remember when you used to steal from their pop machine?"

I quickly answered, "Oh yes, I do, but I confessed all that to God!"

"Yes, you did, but you've never paid them back," the voice insisted.

My newfound peace slowly started drifting away, day after day. I tried to justify that I had confessed everything to God and told Him that I was sorry, but it didn't help. Finally, I realized that confession without restitution is worthless, even though there are wrongs you can't make right because some of the people are already dead and gone.

Look what happened when little Zac came to his senses in Luke 19:8. *"And Zacchaeus stood, and said unto the Lord; behold, Lord, the half of my goods I give to the poor; and if I have taken anything from any man by false accusation, I restore him fourfold."* In the next verse, Jesus said salvation had come to Zacchaeus' house!

Back then, a can of pop was only fifteen cents, so I did the math to figure out how much I'd stolen and multiplied it in that fourfold thing like our friend Zac. Then I jumped into my truck, drove to the place of business, and with trembling, shaky knees, I asked to speak to the owner. I told them what I had done and gave them three crisp twenty-dollar bills, the equivalent of 400, fifteen-cent cans of pop. I really hope the Lord puts some of the extra money on some of my thieving friends' accounts, or better yet, I hope they made their own wrongs right.

Another day, while I was hauling a load of cattle to a distant city, I was dealing with incidents that the Holy Spirit brought to my mind. I said, "God, what do I do with all these peace-stealing issues?" After that, I decided to pick up an old Christian friend, and mile after mile, on a blacktop road somewhere in the USA, I talked and confessed, and he listened. Slowly, the guilt rolled off my shoulders, and my joy became full. I felt like I was floating on beautiful white clouds.

Getting right with your Creator is actually easy! Even a child can grasp this concept: Believe in the finished work of Jesus, that He died for all our sins, and then let His peace be your guide concerning all things in life.

I have learned that the Holy Spirit is kind and gentle. He never gives you more than you can bear, but always a little at a time if you're willing to receive it. Sometimes His work is very painful, by the fruit is joy unspeakable and full of glory! Having perfect peace with God comes from believing in Jesus' finished work and letting the Holy Spirit clean you up from the inside out. *Yes, LORD!*

I've also learned that the devil and his hosts of fallen angels spend all their time accusing the true children of God. They try to make you fall flat on your face, and accuse you when they succeed.

When I was living wildly and carelessly, I wasn't really an outsider with the religious crowd, but I was definitely "in" with the wicked. The religious crowd preached at me, warned me, and warned others about me. They pitied me, but pretty much left me alone. I used to think they would be ecstatic when they heard that I had come to Jesus, believed in Him, and made my peace with God. How wrong I was!

I realized that I had found eternal life in a personal relationship with Jesus, not in the rule book of some denomination. I wanted everyone I knew to have the same peace, joy, and assurance that I had found! I began to reach out to the local community, where many folks believed in JESUS.

Wow, wow, *WOW!* I thought I knew what trouble was when I ran with the wicked, but my eyes were about to be opened, and my mind and heart stretched when I ran up against the concrete wall of religious professors. It's not the average person in a congregation or denomination that causes trouble. It's the professors in charge who feel threatened that cause trouble, division, and fighting. The professors in Jesus' time were so blinded by their jealousy that they wanted to kill Jesus for healing a cripple and a blind man on the Sabbath. No one is as blind as the man who decides not to see when he sees something, and no one is as deaf as the man who refuses to hear something when he hears it.

Everywhere I'd go, the religious zealots would warn people against me and say I was a deceiver, among other things. I'd literally be in someone's home getting ready for an evening preaching session when the fax machine would start rattling with a list of the false things I was supposedly teaching. As the host would hand it to me, he would ask, "Are these accusations true?" Most of them wouldn't be, but that's how gossip and slander is carried abroad. It amazed me how packed the meeting places always were in spite of all the dire warnings folks received against my preaching. I'd hear things like, "Sam teaches that all you need is Jesus. Sam teaches that the Holy Spirit will guide you into all truth. Sam doesn't have authority to baptize but keeps on doing it."

As soon as you make an unreasonable law against something, you give that something a powerful attraction. The Bible tells us that the strength of sin is the law. Google it. This is not meant to be a bitter rant against organized religion. I am only saying that there is a night and day difference between a religious organization with a rule book of "touch not, taste not, handle not standards" and a born-again, Holy Spirit-filled child of God. A religious zealot would love to sin, but tries not to, and a Spirit-filled person doesn't want to sin even though he sometimes does. We're going to be judged by our intentions and why we did what we did.

Jesus came to save the lost, and as many as received Him, to them He gave the power to become the Sons of God. Jesus is the best Friend a sinner could ever find. Long after folks write you off, Jesus is just getting started with you.

Remember, my fine friend; the Romans only did the dirty work for the religious crowd who crucified Jesus because of envy. Yes, the blame lies solely at the professor's door. The beautiful thing is that even the religious professors can repent!

Proverbs 27:4. *Wrath is cruel, and anger is outrageous; but who is able to stand before envy?*

You may not agree with everything I say, but if you live long enough, you'll find these things to be true.

Check out Galatians 1:8-9 *"But though we, or an angel from Heaven, preach any other gospel unto you than that which we have preached unto you, let him be accursed. As we said before, so say I now again, If any man preach any other gospel unto you than that ye have received, let him be accursed."*

Pretty strong words, wouldn't you say?

Now, let me get into the original story!

We were endeavoring to reach into our community to help people, but not everyone appreciated our efforts. I remember one dear soul who would call me up early in the morning before I was out of bed to curse me and falsely accuse me of things that made no sense at all. One particular morning, after receiving a major cursing, I told my wife that the lady had accused me of calling her in the middle of the night. She said she knew it was me harassing her and that she had contacted the police. She admitted that the numbers on the midnight calls were *almost* the same as my number. I tried to explain that I had never called her and that one or two different numbers means it's someone else's phone number, not mine. Still, she insisted that it must have been me. Funny how mixed up your mind can be when you've got it in for somebody. Ha!

One fine spring day shortly after the cursing, and thankfully during the day, I got a call from this same dear lady. "Hello Sam?"

"Yes, ma'am, can I help you?"

"Can you come to my place right away? I need some help!"

"Sure, I'll be right there." I asked my dear wife to pray for me as I headed out the door.

The lady answered the door and said, "I asked a few other people to help me, but they wouldn't, so I got on my knees and asked Jesus what I should do. He told me to call you."

SON OF A SEACOOK

Hmmmmm... "Ok, what can I do for you?"

"My husband left me," she began, opening the cupboards so I could see how empty they all were. "My little girl needs her teeth fixed, and we have no money."

Now, I had just finished building five big pontoon boats, and all my cash flow was tied up. To make matters worse, nothing was selling, and I had an overdraft of 1,800 dollars at my bank, which was a lot in those days. But, I drove to my bank, withdrew 500 dollars, and gave it to the lady. "Oh, thank you, Sam!" she exclaimed tearfully. As I drove away, the voice of reason in my head began like this, "Ya, Sam, that was nice of you, but you know that 500 dollars will barely fix her teeth, let alone put some food on the table? Is that how you'd like someone to treat your wife?"

When Giving Doesn't Make Sense - Pontoon Building

So back I went to my banker and withdrew the remaining amount in my overdraft. My banker said, "That's all your money, Sam."

"I know," I told him. I went back to that lady's house and gave her the rest of that 1,800 dollars.

"I can't accept this without giving you something in return!" the lady said and handed me a nice guitar. "Please take this!"

I drove out of her yard with a nice guitar, but otherwise, I was completely broke. Yet, I felt complete peace. My dear wife met me at the door and wanted to hear all the details. "You mean you emptied our entire account?" she asked wonderingly. "Now what? You know nothing is selling! What are we going to do?"

"I have some room on our credit card," I told her. "I'm going to town to see if I can find some work for some quick cash."

The next morning, I headed out to find a job, and let me tell you, the worry attack was real! I was looking at things from every possible angle and trying not to get too discouraged. Lying beside me was one of the first portable cell phones you had to carry in a large bag because it was cumbersome. Suddenly the phone rang, and my wife said, "Honey, the producers of the Imax movies just called and want to buy a pontoon boat!"

"Now is not a good time for jokes," I told her rather shortly. "I'm really struggling over this whole money issue."

When Giving Doesn't Make Sense - Pontoon Test Drive

"But I'm not joking, Sam. Here's their number."

With shaking hands, I pressed the number keys. "Hello. We're very interested in purchasing one of your boats," said a voice on the other end. "We're shooting a movie on the river up near Brooks, Alberta. Is there any way you could bring one up there tomorrow? We'll pay you for delivering it too."

215

SON OF A SEACOOK

"Yes...yes, I can do that!" I almost shouted.

Early the next morning, I had the boat on the movie site, and they paid me immediately. "Do you have anyone that can operate it for us?" they asked.

"I sure do!" I told them. I called a friend and arranged for him to run the boat and get well-paid while doing it.

My boat ran like a top for them, so the very next day, they bought another one and had me deliver it. Another friend got the job of running it, and again they paid me for the boat and the delivery.

Now get this! They ordered two more boats, so now we had four boats working on the river, bought and paid for, complete with four operators. They told us the name of the movie was *"T-Rex."* If you ever get the chance, you can watch it on IMAX.

A bunch of women were working on the set, doing some heavy lifting, so my men and I pitched in and helped where we could. One of the big shot producers came up to me and said, "We hire these bitches to work, so let them work! No need to help them."

When Giving Doesn't Make Sense - "T-Rex" Filming

Woah...woah...woah!

"A lady needs to be treated like a lady, even if she doesn't act like one," I told him rebukingly.

"Leave them bitches alone!" he retorted. The people on the set asked me why our group was so kind and thoughtful, and even though we had to work hard, we got to share Jesus with them and what He expects of us. They wanted to hear more, so we shared more! They thanked us and said we had reminded them of the important things in life.

How did this go over with the pink-shoed, Hollywood big shot? Not good! If they wouldn't have needed us, we would have been fired on the spot. He actually tried to turn my crew against me, telling them that I should go with the flow and quit messing with people's lives with this Jesus stuff. When my crew told him that they believe just like I do and that we're all on the same team, he just walked away.

When Giving Doesn't Make Sense - On the set of "T-Rex"

As soon as the movie was done, the fellow that bought the pontoon boats came up to me and said, "We don't need these boats anymore, so you might as well take them back home and resell them." We gladly towed them all home. I looked in our bank account, and eighteen thousand dollars was sitting there! Exactly one month after we gave away 1,800! It didn't make sense at the time, but it sure makes sense now! Folks that we had befriended on the set had asked for our address and sent us thank-you letters, complete with meal certificates.

What an awesome God we serve!

Have I doubted since? Yes.
Have I been anxious since? Many, many times.

Why? I don't know.
Am I a super Christian? No.
Do you always know what to do? Absolutely not.
Do you ever get it wrong?? Oh ya!
Why? Because I believe we'll be judged by our intentions, not our actions.

Love, Sam Gary

When Giving Doesn't Make Sense - A tent on a riverboat

ABOUT THE AUTHOR

Sam Gary was born and raised on a large grain farm on the windy prairies of southern Alberta, Canada. He met his wife, Joan Marie (Frey), in Rochester, Minnesota, exactly the halfway point between Alberta, Canada, and Pennsylvania, and together they have raised three daughters and one son.

Sam has always loved new adventures and exploring new business avenues. He has been a hands-on farmer, erected grain bins and feed mills all across Alberta, Saskatchewan, and Manitoba, built pontoon boats, and has obtained his crane operator's license and his pilot's license. He has been a good father, a Bible student, a welder, musician, counselor, and salesman. And all along this amazing journey, he has been writing songs, short stories, and memories of his childhood and growing up years. (Check out Google - The Sam Gary Band Lands in the Top 20 charts, Gets Picked by CMA as 'Who New To Watch in 2009.)

Writing is in his blood because he's always been a storyteller and just can't help himself.

This book, *"Son Of A Seacook,"* is born of memories and laughter and incredible authentic experiences that cry out to be shared with the world. You won't be disappointed.

BIBLIOGRAPHY

BibleGateway. n.d. *1 Kings 17:16.* Accessed 2021.
https://www.biblegateway.com/passage/?search=1+Kings+17%3A16&version=NKJV.

Merritt, Dr. Marlene. 2017. *The Blood Pressure Solution.* Primal Health.

Wikipedia. n.d. *Chinook Wind.* Accessed April 2021.
https://en.wikipedia.org/wiki/Chinook_wind .

Made in the USA
Columbia, SC
25 May 2021